A BURNING CANDLE

The Literary Review
Anthology of Poetry

Copyright (c) The Contributors 1993

ISBN: 1 85731 3364 hardback edition
      1 85731 3313 paperback edition

First published 1993 by
Poetry Now
1 Wainman Road
Peterborough PE2 7BU

LEGAL NOTICE
All rights reserved. No part of this book may be reproduced, stored in a retrieval system, or transmitted in any form, or by any means, electronic, mechanical, photocopying, recording or otherwise, without prior written permission from the publisher.

Cover illustration by William Rushton.

Printed in England by
Forward Press, Peterborough.

Index of Titles

Daughters
Love in an English Garden
Ecstasy
Rats
Collapse of the NHS
London
Greenhouse Effect
New World Order
John Betjeman
Limericks
Housework
Joys of Maturity
Rescue, Relief, Deliverance
Joys of Youth
European Unity
The Poor
Honour and Glory
Hell
A Glimpse of Heaven
Love
A Good Death
Terror
Supernatural Soliciting
First Sighting (Love at First Sight)
Food
Writers Under Socialist Tyranny
Family Album
Wisdom of the World is Foolishness with God
The Ascent of Proserpina
Sloth
Envy and Spite
In Praise of Women

Index

Daughters
The Changeling	Christian Miller	1
Listing Towards You	Frances Wilson	2
Daughters	Paul Griffin	3
The Daughter of Mammon	Herbert Marr	4

Love in an English Garden
Love in an English Garden	Robin Skelton	5
Love in an English Garden	Paul Griffin	7
Love in an English Garden	Robin Skelton	9
The Garden of Chalice-Isle	Herbert Marr	11
Private View	Philip A Nicholson	13

Ecstasy
Ecstasy	Maureen Melvin	14
Landscapes	Alanna Blake	15
Homing	Sarah Spalding	16
Slow-Burn	Kate Lyons	17
Our Cave of Purple Pleasure	Mr and Mrs J Williams	18
Michelangelo's Creation of Man	Frank Mc Donald	19

Rats
Rat Phobia	S Knapp	20
Rat	Sheila McGregor	21
A Postcard	Adelgonda Smit	23
The Water Rat	Anne Jones	25
Unprotected Species	Brian Mitchell	26
The Grey Folk	Joan Butler	27

Collapse of the NHS
Dispensation	Philip A Nicholson	28
The Ward Maid	Paul Griffin	29

London
Mirage	Philip A Nicholson	30
Autumn in London	D A Prince	31
London	Robert Marks	32
London Illusions	Charles Waters	33
Commuters	Alanna Blake	34

Greenhouse Effect
Pennine Miracle	Philip A Nicholson	35
Last Tango in Tooting	Ian Walton	37
An Arrow in the Air	Frank Mc Donald	38
The Greenhouse Effect	Gay Ward	39
The Greenhouse Effect	D A Prince	40
Overexposure	Peter Norman	41

New World Order
Twopence for a Shroud	M Maranka	42
The Friend	Paul Griffin	45
Blank on the Map	Eva Fitzpatrick	46

John Betjeman
John Betjeman - a Tribute	Edward Welby	47
England Needs . . .	Philip A Nicholson	48

Limericks
Limerick	Colin Pearson	49

Housework
What is Housework	Frank Mc Donald	50
Bird with Clipped Wings	Audrey Forbes-Handley	51

Joys of Maturity
Prime Values	Alanna Blake	52
Of Faith Maturing	Frank Mc Donald	53
The Joys of Maturity	Richard Blomfield	54

Rescue Relief Deliverance
In Suspense	Alanna Blake	55
Merciful Release	Helen Forsyth	56
Hostage Crisis	Bill Greenwell	57

Joys of Youth
Sixteen or Natural Selection	Maureen A Jeffs	58
Youth's Intensity	Lindsay Staniforth	59
The Lost Battalion	Paul Griffin	60
Spring Laughter	Frank Mc Donald	61
Youth	Bill Greenwell	62
The Joy of Sex	Katie Mallett	63

European Unity
The Lovely Trains	Robert Perry	64

The Poor
DSS Welcome	Austin Johnson	65
Always With	Katie Mallett	67
Fortune and Men's Eyes	Jenny Morris	69
Rich or Poor	Tim Hopkins	70
Soup Kitchen	Alanna Blake	71
In the Supermarket	D A Prince	72

Honour and Glory
Alan Coren	Philip A Nicholson	73
To Henry Vaughan, Who needs no Praise	Don Rodgers	74
In Honour . . . Philip Bourke-Marston	C F Marfell-Harris	75

Hell
Hell	Elizabeth Imlay	76
Kenealy's Version	Noel Petty	77
Hell, a New Eternity	Katherine Turner	78

A Glimpse of Heaven
A Glimpse Beyond the Veil	Frank Mc Donald	79
To a Beloved Robin	Maureen Jeffs	81
The Shaft of Light	Stella Browning	82
And Let the Credit go	Philip A Nicholson	83

Love
To my Wife	Allan Warbis	84
A Literate Love	Patricia V Dawson	85
To my (School) Mistress	Paul Griffin	86
Stigmata	Helen Chown	87
To X	Jill Neville	88

A Good Death
A Good Death	Myfanwy Lloyd	89
A Good End	Paul Griffin	91
Good Death	Charles Porter	92
Death of Deaths	Philip A Nicholson	93
Mercy	Alanna Blake	94
A Good Death	D A Prince	95

Terror
Terror	Richard Graves	96

Supernatural Soliciting
After Death	D A Prince	97
Doppelganger	Tim Hopkins	98
House of the Dead	Roger Caldwell	99
Déjà-Vu	Elizabeth Sadik	101

First Sighting (Love at First Sight)
Commuter Train	Barbara Balch	102
First Sighting	Mortimer Spreader	103
To Annabel	Edward Welby	105
The New Neighbour	G R Harvey	106

Food
Food, Glorious Food	Alison Prince	107
Plea Bargain	Philip A Nicholson	108

Writers Under Socialist Tyranny
A Russian Poet Laments His Freedom	Noel Petty	109
Togrop	Allan Warbis	110
Life's Persecution	Frank Mc Donald	111

Family Album
With Wild Flowers For my Father's Grave	Angus Sinclair	112
Family Albums	Philip A Nicholson	113
The Widow's Table	Roger Caldwell	114
In Memoriam	Richard Charles	115

Wisdom of the World is Foolishness with God
Mens Insana	H St G Cramp	116
Foolishness With God	Frank Mc Donald	117
A Fool's Response	Alex Smith	118

The Ascent of Proserpina
Cur Venisti, Proserpina?	Frank Mc Donald	119
Inner City Primavera	Jenny Morris	121
Proserpina Discouraged	Patricia V Dawson	122
And Still Persephone Returns	Maureen A Jeffs	123
Overdue	Brian Mitchell	124

Sloth
Sloth: a Theory	Noel Petty	125
Darling	Ralph Stephenson	126
The Sloth	Victoria Thompson	127
Not Today	D A Prince	128
England	Robert Marks	129
Ode to Idleness	Richard Charles	130

Envy and Spite

The Poetry, Not the Poet	Robert Hart	131
Spite and Envy	Bill Greenwell	133
The Great McGongall	Robert Marks	134
John Keats	D A Prince	135
The Price of Envy	Patricia V Dawson	136

In Praise of Women

A Qualified Toast	Patricia V Dawson	137
The Wife	Richard Blomfield	138
Footnotes	David Shields	139

A BURNING CANDLE

The Literary Review Anthology of Poetry

Introduction
by
AUBERON WAUGH

Shortly after the first *Literary Review* anthology of poetry came out I went to Birmingham to publicise the book on a Central Television chat show called, I think, *Friday Night*, or something of the sort. It is done in front of a studio audience rather like *Question Time*, except that whereas the *Question Time* audiences are specially chosen to represent various points of view and organised pressure groups - the *Friday Night* audience was, so far as one could judge, a genuine slice of Birmingham opinion.

The idea was that modern poets would read from their work, after which I would read the poem which won our first annual Grand Poetry Prize of £5,000, sponsored by the *Mail on Sunday* in 1990 - Frank Mc Donald's *Of Seas and Galleons* and the audience would then debate the whole vexed question of whether poetry is better if it rhymes, scans and makes sense.

One of the 'modern' camp, a young man whose name I have lost, read an extraordinarily banal composition about the Gulf War, which was then about to break out. He read in a deeply sincere voice and was heard respectfully - rather as people used to listen respectfully to prayers being read in the days when religion was thought normal, rather than an eccentric minority enthusiasm.

The other modernist was my old friend Horowitz or Horovitz (as he prefers). Horowitz simply stuck some feathers in his bottom and hopped around the studio crowing like a cock. Needless to say, he was rapturously received. Thunderous cheers broke out and it was obvious who the favourite was.

I have never flattered myself that I am a particularly good reader aloud of poetry, but when I started reading Frank Mc Donald's memorable poem -

> Sunset galleon, sunset galleon, moving through a dreamer's ocean
> Let them label you illusion or an old man's foolish notion,
> But the waves on which you shiver surely lead towards a heaven
> To a seaside, to a childhood in which faults are all forgiven.

- I was disappointed to observe an audience reaction which consisted of emanations not so much of indifference or boredom, as of plain hostility. This might have been ascribable to my fruity voice, whose accents an entire generation of Englishmen have been trained to loathe, but the debate later revealed a settled antipathy to poetry which rhymed and scanned. They said they thought it old fashioned and outmoded, but what I think they meant was that they found it an oppressive reminder of an English society which existed before they came into their own - before, that is, *vox populi* became identified as *vox Dei*. What they were saying, I fancy, was that modern poetry may be rubbish but at least it belonged to them. Frank Mc Donald's swaying rhythm, full of classical allusions and metaphysical concerns, belonged to an alien, educated culture for which they did not care and which could no longer frighten them. More particularly, any reminder of its existence demanded a stern reaction which might be seen as social or historical revenge, or might be seen as just punishment for the crimes of snobbery and élitism.

It was salutary to learn that *Literary Review's* attempt to keep a lamp burning through the Dark Ages was not only against the grain of contemporary fashion, but also deeply unpopular with the man in the street. I had thought otherwise, relying on the enormous popular success of such enterprises as *Poems on the Underground*, which combines old favourites from the past with less 'difficult' Tom and Jerry-style contemporaries. But plainly the matter needs exploring. My guess is that the appetite for reasonably proper poetry survives, so long as it is presented in a laid-back way. But it must not be so laid-back as to antagonise the educated, intelligent audience to which it is addressed.

It came as no surprise that the first anthology, published in 1990, received scarcely a single review in any newspaper or magazine. Of the two *Telegraphs*, the two *Timeses*, the two *Independents*, the *Guardian*, the *Observer*, the *Financial Times*, *Spectator*, *New Statesman*, nearly all have poetry editors on whose judgement the literary editor relies. One would have thought that an earnest attempt by one of England's three literary publications to restore formal poetry, introducing some sixty new poets, might have excited some comment in those quarters which are entirely dedicated to commenting on the poetry scene - even if only to say that it had failed. Their refusal to mention it indicates more than hostility. I would like to think that it indicates terror - or at any rate a profound unease.

If the contemporary poetry establishment is judged by what it produces, we must decide it is in a very abject state indeed. The early days of the Modern Movement, when it was breaking new ground, were marked by a creative vitality which attracted bold, talented pioneers. Now, of course, it is in the hands of the tired, the second-rate, the cynical and the manipulators of government grants. If our humane, liberal, bourgeois culture were not in itself disappearing under the new culture of mass entertainment, these people might have been turned off their perches long ago. As it is, they cling on, summoning just enough kindergarten or happy-clappy enthusiasm among the simple-minded to persuade themselves that they have a purpose.

I cannot make extravagant claims for the poems in this book. Some are better than others, and some are really not at all bad, but none possesses that mysterious quality of Shelley's *Ozymandias*, perhaps, or Tennyson's *The Eagle*, which makes you feel it should be familiar to every man, woman and child in the country. The poets' predicament, as I see it, is that the English language is already surfeited with good poetry. So, it might be said, is the Western world surfeited with good music, but then there is also a limit to the number of melodies possible. In the same way the painter has had a large part of his primary function destroyed by the camera, the novelist (as storyteller) has been overtaken by cinema and television, the sculptor is frustrated to some considerable extent by the banality of modern dress and the vulgarisation of the nude form. Modern life, perhaps, does not wish to be memorialised. It is worrying enough to know how to dispose of all these bodies, without having to record their existence.

But poets have no such excuse. There is no solid reason why they cannot write poetry based on their own experiences, feelings and observation which is as beautiful and wise as Shakespeare's. Our language is essentially the same. All that prevents us from trying is a sort of millennial laziness - call it *accidie* or *noia*, or spleen, or any fancy word you choose. It is because they know that what they are protecting is worthless that the guard-dogs of the poetry establishment are so bitter, secretive and silent.

At the time of writing, the Literary Review's monthly Grand Poetry Competition continues to be generously sponsored by Messrs Biddle and Company, the noted City solicitors. Once a year, we have a £5,000 prize for the best poem published in the last twelve months. This, at present, is sponsored by the Mail on Sunday. Every month I set a subject - it might be the End of a Love Affair, or Rats, or Persephone's Ascent from the Underworld. Entries must rhyme, scan and make sense on the subject set. They may be no longer than 30 lines, and competitors are restricted to a maximum of two entries. It cost nothing to enter, but the monthly first prize of £350 and second prize of £150 are restricted to subscribers. Other prizes are usually available, and £10 is paid for all poems printed. Parody and pastiche are not eligible for first prize. Subscription details, and copies of the magazine, may be obtained from Literary Review at 51 Beak Street, London W1R 3LF.

Copies of the first volume Literary Review's Anthology of Real Poetry (Buchan and Enright 1990) are completely sold out and unobtainable. I would be delighted to hear from anyone who has a spare copy. Finally, heartfelt thanks to the editor, Dariane Pictet and the twelve strong Poetry Panel of which she is a member, for their prodigious, unrewarded efforts.

Dear Editor,
  You are a fool
To institute the petty rule
That puts an arbitrary ban
On verse that doesn't rhyme or scan!
Free verse, in good hands, can be taut,
Elliptical and finely wrought;
Who knows what masterpieces are
Excluded by this foolish bar?
Four hundred pounds a month could be
A prize for *proper* poetry -
Not thrown away on lightweight lines
Like February's Valentines
Tossed off by refugee technicians
From certain other competitions.
I am a double fool, you say,
For thinking thus, and for the way
I follow slavishly that rule
I rail against. Not so! A fool
Is one who, confidently wise,
Knows not where his best interest lies.
We all have flaws - ah, yes indeed!
While yours is folly, mine is greed.

Peter Norman

Editor's Note

As in the Chinese saying; 'The wise man points to the moon, the fool looks at the finger', the poet ideally attempts to formulate into words the reflection of a mystery, a truth that can only be glimpsed but which echoes deep within us, like a ripple across the water reminds us that a stone was thrown. Some do it with more grace than others. Restrictions imposed here were the rhyming and scanning rule, a set subject announced every month and an outside time limit of thirty days. They have not silenced the Muse.

Some subjects were very inspiring while others didn't work so well. 'Daughters', 'Rats', 'Family', 'Ecstasy', 'Love in an English Garden', 'Rescue', 'London', fired the imagination, 'Housework' and 'The Collapse of the NHS', perhaps predictably didn't. Surprisingly neither did 'Love of Food'.

There was a variety in the standard of poems between years; 90/91 was excellent. Almost all the subjects cited above come from that year, where as there was a definite lack of inspiration in 91/92. It wasn't a bad year just for the Queen it seems. However it gave us 'Joys of Youth', 'Hell' and 'The Poor', among others. 92/93 started well with 'Supernatural Soliciting', but didn't really pick up again until 'Ecstasy' around the middle of the year. After that we were on a roll. Politics, recession, choice of subjects as well as the panel could be determining factors.

Poets come and go; apart from a few reliable authors, who seem to provide us with a steady crop throughout, the vast majority of poets are new to this anthology since only 13 poets from the last one are represented here.

The Changeling

My daughter sat beside me at the glass;
We talked of trivial things, of what she'd wear,
Of who would be there at the dance that night.
Her fingers smoothed her shining, silken hair.

She nothing has of me, I thought,
(Her golden head so close against my brow)
Her very eyebrows have a different slant,
Her cheeks and lips are utterly her own.

Those lips, that clung once closely to my breast
And cried for me, now with another reap
A sweeter consolation than I sowed. In other arms
The future holds for her a sounder sleep.

I was but instrument to give her birth,
She cast me off, and nothing took of me,
No single feature, touch of tears or mirth,
No gesture, nothing that the eye could see.

The doorbell rang below. She spun around
And suddenly, trapped by surprise,
Reflected in the glass, my own transmitted
Soul shone at me from her eyes.

Christian Miller

Listing Towards You
(To my daughter, on leaving home.)

I write my lists to keep life's storms at bay.
Without them the horizon looms too wide.
Their weathered words protect my tidal day,

Create a tranquil anchorage to ride.
While yours are used as ballast, so you say;
Without their weight you drift from side to side,
Aimless and starless in uncharted sea.
I watch your steady course and think with pride -
Such a short time ago, you moored to me.

Frances Wilson

Daughters

Two daughters made an ancient king
A byword for his suffering;
Just the unexpected third
Offered him a loving word.

Which shall represent the norm,
Those who drove him to the storm
Or the daughter who was sweet
In the darkness of defeat?

Rather ask what father could
Tell his bad ones from his good;
Fathers now, like King Lear then,
All are foolish fond old men.

Love your daughters, not for grace,
Not for virtue, nor for face;
Unconditionally kind,
Honour Lear for being blind.

Paul Griffin

The Daughter of Mammon

To give her speech richness and worth,
She placed a pound beneath her tongue;
Another pressed into each palm
So reach of money might be long.

That all the world might know her wealth
She strapped a gold coin to her chest,
To keep her body firm yet flat,
Two round coins pressed hard at each breast.

Resisting love and common things,
She hid a coin between her thigh
That in that rich and fertile space
It might grow fat and multiply.

To stay in sight before her gaze,
One coin was fastened to her nose;
Beneath her feet were two coins more:
Reminders of the road she chose.

Above her head, well balanced, still,
One small gold coin flashed in her hair
And kept her eyes from looking down -
Or looking up with wondering stare.

Oh, daughter of the world, how sad
This offspring of your metal loin:
You've vanquished all the tenderness
Bequeathed by love's more gentle coin.

Herbert Marr

Love in an English Garden
(A Sicilian Quintet)

That vicarage garden with its croquet lawn
and long skirts brushing the shorn daisied grass,
the leg-of-mutton sleeves, the piled hats worn
sedately, calm; our days cannot surpass
that vicarage garden with its croquet lawn,

the plink of shuttlecock on battledores,
the feathers spiralling into the blue
asserting happiness that spins and soars
above the trembling net, the me, the you,
the plink of shuttlecock on battledores.

These are delights whose loss we well might mourn
who, sipping gin beneath the chestnut trees,
contrive a courtship fashion can't adorn
with flounces, furbelows, and fripperies
these are delights whose loss we well might mourn

but that we understand those ageless laws
of perpetuity: nothing ever dies.
Around us long gone lovers gesture, pause,
flirt, kiss, embrace, agree, and could surprise
but that we understand those ageless laws

as, in our love, ancestral faith's reborn,
a faith the topiary and the roses know,
a faith in order and in plenty's horn,
and wisdom's move around us, gentle, slow,
as, in our love, ancestral faith's reborn.

That vicarage garden with its croquet lawn,
the plink of shuttlecock on battledores -
these are delights whose loss we well might mourn
but that we understand those ageless laws
as, in our love, ancestral faith's reborn.

Robin Skelton

Love in an English Garden

We loved, how many years ago?

So thoroughly we seem to know
The shapes of these autumnal trees,
The patterned shade, the sound of bees,
The garden perfumes on the air,
The lawn, the light, the leaves, and there
The crumpled water of the pool,
Casually beautiful -
So thoroughly, we half forget
The circumstances in which we met,

When each on each was so intent
We could not see what gardens meant.

Love is not gone, but it has grown
Aware of growth itself, has known
How autumn crocus, golden rod,
Can turn our grateful hearts to God
And help this perfect place to prove
A living witness to our love.

Yet autumn brings another smell,
An ancient message we know well:
Compost and wood smoke, rotten plums,
Wet grass, and old chrysanthemums,
A choir of smells that faintly sings
A requiem for living things.

This winter compost that we scent
Is food for life's replenishment;
But what of love? When we are dead
Can it remain, and raise its head
Triumphantly, some future spring,
With every other living thing?

How may we hope to find this place
When time has turned away her face?

Paul Griffin

Love in an English Garden
(Another Sicilian Quintet)

Our love will last the summer out;
just as this garden will endure
the sun, the wind, the rain without
uncertainties, we may be sure
our love will last the summer out.

Within the shadows of the trees
we, Berkeley-like, compose our day;
without us, butterflies and bees
would be no more than shapes that play
within the shadows of the trees.

Why bother what the world's about,
that alien world our love has banned,
the world of riot, wrath, and rout?
As my hand reaches to your hand,
why bother what the world's about?

No hours are as calm as these
of summer and the roses' pride,
their silken petals speaking case;
however many men have died,
no hours are as calm as these,

no loves less modified by doubt,
for we have altered earth and air,
renewed the fire, the sea, devout
in reverence for the gods, and swear
no love's less modified by doubt.

Our love will last the summer out
within the shadows of the trees.
Why bother what the world's about?
No hours are as calm as these,
no loves less modified by doubt.

Robin Skelton

The Garden of Chalice-Isle

I know an ancient garden by a wall
Where steady smiles and firm resolve ascend:
A gentle glade of hidden happiness
Set in a land where peace and honour tend.

Here in this peaceful, green-secluded isle,
Bright star-kissed lovers softly serenade;
No wrecking anger steals their scented air
Nor with'ring years their promises can jade.

Within this ground of compassed dignity
Eternal lovers' moods are new expressed;
Encouragements through structured praise exchanged,
And dreams, through still and quiet hope, addressed.

Enriching joy is shared in murmurings;
Each passing comment heard is positive;
High fluting birds and heavy, fragrant blooms
Suggest Chalice-Isle's way is how to live.

A cleanly flowing river of delight
Resounds with bubbling tunes exuberant;
Strong fountains of pure laughter richly play,
Requiring nothing mean or petulant.

This glade shall form the centre of my earth:
Here weary men may pause and grow refreshed;
Here simple dreamers strengthen their resolve
To leave confusion in its web enmeshed;

Here, misery and sullenness must pause
And wait on peace. Then, like a gentle bell,
Its peeling music can refresh the soul
Till suffering shall cease at this deep well.

Its English fragrances perfume the world
And spread by contact to diminish pain,
Till all that mess of sad humanity
Can echo to its laughter once again.

Herbert Marr

Private View

There is a garden that I know
Where blooms of gentler ages grow,
A living sanctuary of calm
And elegant Edwardian charm,
Where stippled turf and woodland glade
Meet cool mosaics of light and shade,
Where diamond latticed waters run
Through valleys drenched in summer sun
And pinnacled gazebos rise
To meet eternal English skies.

This is the refuge where I go
When life's affairs have laid me low
A private garden of the soul
That makes my fractured spirit whole,
There is no death within its gate,
No pain or strife, no fear or hate
But only love, and that deep peace
That gives tormented man release,

And so, I do not fear or dread
Whatever fate may lie ahead,
For I am privileged to see
The paradise that is to be.

Philip A Nicholson

Ecstasy

It wasn't when you offered to escort me down the aisle;
It wasn't when I bore your son and saw his infant smile;
It wasn't when you bought for me the cottage of my dreams,
Complete with death-watch beetle and the woodworm in the beams.

It wasn't when you praised me for my triumph as your cook,
Nor even when the publisher agreed to take my book.

No, ecstasy at last was mine - oh, memorable coup!
The day I first was published in the *Literary Review*.

Maureen Melvin

Landscapes

The mountain peaks of ecstasy are really for the young:
the sweaty rise, the awkward leap, the sharp salt on the tongue;
seductive dangers lurking in the plummet of the falls,
endearments voiced as artlessly as curlews' mating calls,
co-operative scrambles onto some climactic top,
to a dizzy panorama when the upward pantings stop.

So give me now the easy walk, the flat familiar plain,
the river flowing slowly and bright daylight on the wane,
as quiet moving shadows frame a soft, near-sighted view
of subtle modulations where disturbances are few.
However consciously I choose these lowland calms, it seems
the mountain peaks of ecstasy still dominate my dreams.

Alanna Blake

Homing

Why at the season's ebb am I so full,
So brimming at the wall I run and run
Against the flow, against the slow, sad pull
Of Autumn as she gathers in the sun?
Yours is the open shore I break upon
Where lonely gulls hoist up their jagged cry,
Where shingle rolls a Celtic orison,
Where all my driftwood miseries run dry.

Stranded from you, escapes the rebel child,
A lady of misrule who storms the age,
Howls blind the harvest moon, is helpless, wild
And captive to each dying minute's rage.
Wrapped up in you my tides run like the sea,
Incessant and voluptuous and free.

Sarah Spalding

Slow-Burn

My first love - seventeen and, oh, so pretty.
One blissful day I sat beside him - close
Beside him in the train to school . . . The pity
Was it happened only once in all those
Doting years. And we didn't smile or touch
Or exchange a word. But no journey since
Has passed so hopefully, concealed such
Transports of rapture in cool indifference.

And all that August idle by the river
A dozen of us lazed and swam, displayed
Tumbling together in grass and water, aquiver
In a web of could and might but not one strayed
From innocence; though, tuned to the siren's song,
We coasted, circling, skirting consummation.
Ecstasy shimmered throughout that summer-long,
Subdued slow-burn of expectation.

Kate Lyons

Our Cave of Purple Pleasure

I walked with my girl on a warm hillside
Till we came to a mass of tangled brier.
Piercing this confusion with purple pride
Were ranks of foxgloves, dappled with desire.
The sun poured honey on the foxgloves' bells,
The bees hummed and hovered before drinking
The nectar of life, which always compels -
'You must do it today without thinking!'
We too have our cave of purple pleasure,
But ours has cunning curtains, sweet to touch.
We probed and explored its trembling treasure
- No other gift could ever give so much.
Soaked with satisfaction, I was beguiled;
She caught my glance, and lazily she smiled.

Mr and Mrs J Williams

Michelangelo's Creation of Man

Is it so hard to think that God allowed
A favoured soul to see beyond the shroud,
Guided his fingers to adorn a ceiling
With genius love, with ecstasies of feeling,
In mortal ways? Thus does that finger reach
Across time's gap, thus does it all but touch
The perfect moment of our reveries,
And we how bridge the bridgeless centuries,
Are naked Adams raised, renaissance-style,

Towards God's truth. In unison we smile,
He in the flesh of time we cannot know,
We in our present . . . Michelangelo,
Saints have been made from less,
Who fashioned love from suffering and distress,
Who found their God in penances and prayer,
Turning their eyes to wild and empty air,
Searching the skies for trace of seraphim.
But you surpassed the blindness of their hymn,
Sweeping aside the chains of guilt and lust,
Offering God not diadems but dust,
And He who fathered flesh well understood
The lonely splendour of your nameless nude,
Granting him purpose, sovereignty, power
To conquer life. In that poetic tower
Painted above the sighs of monarchy,
Behold a man in god-like ecstasy.

Frank Mc Donald

Rat Phobia

'Good evening, dear,' she kissed his nose
Then looked behind and body froze
With terror causing trembling sides
And tears balanced on panicked eyes.
'Look there!' she whispered, scarcely heard,
With voice composed of snuffling word.

He turned and gasped then stiffened cold
Paralysed by fear's rock hold.
'Don't move!' he cried, 'he'll go away,
Thank God we move next Saturday.'

Intruder left, the couple sighed
Then ate their meal alert, wide eyed
In soft, warm room with orange glow
Of gentle light kept homely low.

'They're dirty things,' he spat in spite,
'They rarely wash, they ever fight,
They're primitive, they spread disease,'
He stroked his whiskers, 'Pass the cheese.'

S Knapp

Rat

Just lately, I've become aware
Of your patient, pink-eyed stare.
I think, as I am passing by,
I think you try to catch my eye.

I pass the others without thought.
But passing you my eye is caught.
Number zero, stroke, two three
I feel you're trying to contact me.

Each night when shedding my white coat
I think of yours. How you devote
Such time and care. You lick and groom,
While mine goes to the laundry room.

As I swab, then pierce your vein
And drip you drugs that cause you pain,
I find I can no longer bear
Your suffering. I find I care.

Today's the day. You're on my list
To go to the pathologist.
I cannot take you through that door.
I've substituted stroke, two four.

Security is very hot,
But even so they didn't spot
You nestled quietly in my pocket
As I signed my exit docket.

So now I keep you by my bed,
So bright, alive instead of dead.
I let you free to seek and roam
To learn to know your strange new home.

My wife was screaming yesterday.
She couldn't see that it was play
When you, you tinker, tried to gnaw
An entrance through her wardrobe door.

She's gone now. Said you made her quail
With naked feet, and scaly tail.
I've lost my job because of you.
I'm up in court. They're going to sue.

But now I sit here on my own.
Jobless, broke and all alone.
To think that after all of that
You made a meal for next door's cat!

Sheila McGregor

A Postcard

Dear Rat. I thought I'd drop a line.
Remember me? We met that fine
Late summer afternoon. You sat
Beside the dusty road. Another Rat
(Yes! It was I!) lay down to rest.
I told my story, told my endless quest
For southern climates, and the foam
Of azure waters, far from home.
You brought a picnic; and we spoke
About your River, and the folk
Who live along the Riverbank;
Of feuds and feastings, and of boats that sank.
And are your pals all well? I trust
That Toad's alive; for all his lust
For Motor-cars, I like him best,
Gaitered and goggled, in his lemon vest.
He had a taste for life, unlike the Mole,
Such an old woman, primping up his hole
With whitewash, carpet slipper shod
Creeping about like some furred gastropod.
He was a sponger too, I always thought
Eating the victuals which you bought and bought.
Stubborn and witless, only he would go

Alone, at night, into the coming snow
And lose himself in that Wild Wood.
And Mr Badger? Ever great and good?
I feared him most. I know this sort:
A steely Captain; as in every port
A Magistrate I'd find like him,
Ready to whip us sea-rats on a whim.
And Otter? do the pipes still play
Softly before the rosy dawn of day
As when you found his little boy
Beside Pan's feet, in awesome joy.

I have no god: the sea's my all
Its ebb and flow has me in thrall.
Rat! You should have come with me
I would have shown you such a life at sea.
The water's salty and the ship is old
And fear and hunger haunt the dismal hold.
There is a Cat. It creeps like Care
Into our dreams, with glassy stare!
And yet! and yet! I could not go
To where your sweet winds softly blow.
As subtle as a poisoned glove
We bring the plague to those you love.

Adelgonda Smit

The Water Rat

Whispered rustling in the rush ringed
Flesh flagged fringes of the lake.
Velvet movements in the shadows -
V-formationed water wake.

Clockwork piston legs dog-paddle,
Bulldoze shoulders aquaplane.
Head erect - determination
Bristles through the stocky frame.

Black eyes fixed, no deviation
Seems to catch the rigid gaze -
Dead-straight furrow ploughs forever
In the rising evening haze.

Oiled and leak-proof, russet coated,
Nostrils fastened for the dive,
Flat-eared, smooth and neatly gliding,
Whiplash-tailed - torpedo drive.

Trails of bubbles bursting upwards;
Sunflash strings of diamond gems.
Sharply snapping white incisors
Slice the water-lily stems.

Pinioned panic in the reed bed,
Freeze frame flash of tousled head.
Brent geese, jumbo-jetting take-off,
Wing whirl, feet beat, water tread.

Scrambling bank-climb, fur shake shower,
Tail squat, coat sleek, whisker comb,
Water rat, re-lubricated,
Snuggles safe in dark holed home.

Anne Jones

Unprotected Species

Six new-born rats, pink, helpless, blind,
Milk-drowsy from her paps,
A hungry mother leaves behind
And forages for scraps.

Suspicion twitching whiskered snout,
She snuffles left and right
As warily she darts about
Prepared for instant flight.

She ventures on to open ground,
Too far for safe retreat,
And from above, without a sound,
Death strikes with taloned feet.

In hollow elm four fledglings wait,
The barn owl's latest brood,
And, scenting fresh-killed meat, they bate,
Each clamouring for food.

Now motherless, the litter dies,
Whilst round-eyed nestlings thrive,
Yet who would care to moralise
As long as owls survive?

Brian Mitchell

The Grey Folk

(There is an old belief in the Isle of Man that to speak of rats in anything other than euphemistic terms is to summon them)

Misty creatures of Mannanan,
   Wisps of shadow, wraiths of smoke,
Glimpse us in the sea fret's drifting,
In and out of vision shifting,
Through his rocky fingers sifting,
   Darting underneath his cloak.

Greedy men who seized this island,
   We were here before you came.
Here we flourish still, despite you,
(Spite and devilment requite you!)
And will haunt you, plague you, blight you,
   Should you call us by our name.

Call us - if you will - the Grey Folk,
   Would you have up keep away;
Call on ancient superstitions,
Babbling witches, grave magicians,
Call us twilight apparitions,
   Call us fairy, call us fay.

Call us pest, we will not harm you;
   Call us vermin, call us scum:
In the darkness, in the gutter,
Eyes blood-red and claws a-scutter,
Marking every word you utter -
   Calls us Rats, and we will come.

Joan Butler

Dispensation

The erstwhile horn of plenty
Offers plenitude no more,
In meagre draughts Hippocrates
Doles out a dwindling store,
The old, the impecunious,
Gaze with unbelieving eyes
As inscrutable computers
Decide who lives or dies.
Odd unlikely transplants
Are the order of the day
While sore afflicted multitudes
Are daily turned away.
And as our crumbling NHS
With all its broken dreams
Subsides beneath the rising tide
Of debt and private schemes,
Profligate technicians
Await with bated breath
The ultimate achievement . . .
An antidote for death.

Philip A Nicholson

The Ward Maid

At the first light she sweeps the midnight out,
The broken pot, the scattered lees of tea,
Tangible echoes of a frightened shout,
A crisis met, but not with urgency.

The moaning dark, when someone seemed to die,
Lies in a heap of scraps upon the floor,
Leaving a weary girl to sweep and sigh
And bang her brush's head against the door.

A trolley brings the new day's breakfast smells;
She and the sun have done their task again,
Effaced that clumsy night among the bells
That rang and rang, but failed to ease the pain.

Paul Griffin

Mirage

A legendary city
  circulates within my head,
Buildings I have never seen
  streets I shall not tread,
Fragrant Chelsea mornings,
  Dickens' alleyways of crime,
'Sweet Thames running softly'
  'sylvan Kew in lilac time'
Flash of sabres in the sunlight,
  nodding plumes and prancing steeds,
All the images of London
  that romanticism breeds.
But alas, I fear to visit
  for as every cynic knows,
Careful scrutiny reveals
  the canker in the rose,
So I cherish my illusions
  and worship from afar,
Better dream-defended castles
  than a ruined Shangri-La.

Philip A Nicholson

Autumn in London

London is for lovers. Not the young -
Parading promises in full brash lust -
But softer, secret, sad-eyed couples sprung
From suburb traps, from marriages where rust

Stains and corrodes fidelity. They meet
In Finsbury Circus, under sooty trees,
Or windy corners off Great Russell St,
Or in museums' marbled galleries -

Egyptian or Assyrian: all the same.
Know them by their concerned fragility,
Their bird's-eye nervousness, and ghost of blame:
Their knowledge of the small streets of the city,

Twining their twin geographies around
The softly-running Thames: sad, drooping planes
In autumn on the Embankment, with the sound
Of mocking barges. Holborn rains

Sweep them for shelter into Lincoln's Inn:
October sun, and sparrowed Russell Square,
Brittle with leaf-ribs, autumn's bulletin,
Gives them a moment's capital, to share

London's unwritten history. The tears
Shed in Victoria, or Chancery Lane
Slide fast-forgotten down the larger years -
Wars, governments, the public world's domain -

But underneath the postcards' images -
Buckingham Palace, what the tourist sees,
The changing guards - are unchanged tragedies,
All London's private anonymities.

D A Prince

London

Past the Globe and Paris Garden
Beckoned by the Bow bells' peal,
There the tracks of iron harden
Into streets of tangled steel.

Brutish helmeted tormentors
Stand on guard at city gates,
No one unencumbered enters
Every prospect aggravates.

Hordes of tourists by the hour
Hurry on their pilgrimage,
Executions at the Tower
Severed heads on London Bridge.

Set between construction messes
Sprouting blocks of glass and chrome,
Ugly pile of Wren's excesses
Sulks beneath its bogus dome.

Robert Marks

London Illusions

I travelled down to London,
A country lad, and green,
To see the streets where pleasure greets
A youth of seventeen.

I hurried from the station
Impatient to explore;
The diamond sparks in squares and parks
Held wisdom, wealth and more.

Vast concrete blocks around me
Where life went on unseen,
Invited me to come and see,
When I was seventeen.

And here was Piccadilly,
With lights like sparkling eyes,
I gazed around, soul filled with sound,
At life, at love, at lies.

With pride I walked down Bond Street,
Enthused around Park Lane,
I stopped to stare on Leicester Square
For I was foolish then.

Cold statues now despise me,
And mock what dreams survive,
A London day is noisy, grey,
Now I am twenty five.

Charles Waters

Commuters

'All tickets ready!' Each weekday, same seat,
Joined by the overlapping of the Times,
The camouflage of morning smoke complete,
They grunt their greeting wordlessly as mimes;
Eyes slide from faces on to shifting feet,
Jerk to the rattle of diverging lines;
Sharing so many hours, they never meet.

'Move right along inside!' The pressing queue
Carries them without effort up the stair,
Forces them roughly into spaces too
Narrow for comfort, seats them pair by pair.
Linked above city traffic for these few
Minutes until bells chime, the bus stop's where
Neighbours' unnoticed faces pass from view.

'Mind the doors please!' Wait for the start to fling
Bodies that strike a balance thigh to thigh,
Cuffs gently kissing, hands in a single ring,
Breaths of relief in one concerted sigh;
Touch becomes neutered, each is just a thing
Filling the void a journey must imply.
Armed by nonentity they clutch and cling.

Alanna Blake

Pennine Miracle

Where once the wizened hawthorn
Crooked its fingers at the sky,
The fragrant jacaranda
Beguiles the passer-by;
Piercing our obscurity
Revealing radiance falls,
Not on slated rooftops
Lichened rock and blackened walls
But on Tuscan terracotta
Pastelled stone and stuccoed white,
Suffusing grey antiquity
With pools of warmth and light.

On hillsides lately barren
Proliferates the vine,
In market-place and hostelry
The talk is all of wine
From patio and sprinklered lawn
The bright umbrellas sprout
The trendy tropic look is 'in'
And Northerns dourness 'out';
Antibes has come to Lancashire,
Down alleyway and street,
The tipsy tourist patters by
On dark brown sandalled feet.

Antibes has come to Lancashire
They're dancing in the squares,
On sun-soaked sands the seaside bands
Play continental airs,
Antibes has come to Lancashire!
Why then am I not glad!
Why amid euphoria
Am I uniquely sad!

True, I feel as others do
That balmy tropic breeze,
But though it warms my skin it fills
My soul with cold unease.

Philip A Nicholson

Last Tango in Tooting

As global warming took its grip
and passions rose with every tide,
mad dogs roamed the streets at noon:
inhibitions pushed aside,
daring all, we took the chance
to exorcise our temperance
and ventured to the office dance.

Dribbling libido down his leg,
a languid Latin tapped my arm,
wrapped himself around my wife,
whispered 'may I' and oozing charm
slid her across the polished boards,
between the tanned and tainted hordes
of Arab-Geordies from up north.

The band struck up in double time:
I stiffened as a paramour's
soft hand explored my inner thigh;
my wife was writhing on the floor
with a lizard of a man
(sporting a Llanelli tan)
who looked a lot like Genghis Khan.

The buffet stank of kiwi fruit
and melons, grown in Inverness,
that sun-kissed maids from Sutherland
proffered to guests. I must confess,
I had no reason to suspect
the ozoneless greenhouse effect
would propagate such wanton sex.

Ian Walton

An Arrow in the Air

You watch them through the fractured ozone layer,
Amused at Adam's progeny, and thrilled
At your strands of wisdom drifting in the air,
Delighted that your plan has been fulfilled
In every sunbeam, every drop of rain,
If only mutant man would comprehend;
Yet do they read the lines you wrote in vain?
They aerosol their faith, and fear the end.

But in each waning moon, each scorching sun
You breathed a whisper of a wiser plan;
There is the thought that life will labour on
Despite the petty purposes of man
Whose silly arrow, puncturing the air,
Will fall again to earth, no damage done;
No fires, no floods will generate despair,
Seasons will change, and centuries will run.

You smile upon the ignorance of pride
That fears it may frustrate your primal pen,
But knowing what millennia you hide
You let them play, and chuckle you amen
As they blow a cloud or two across the sky.
And if the toys they build should heat the earth
You'll yawn a godly yawn, and bye and bye,
They'll realise their works have little worth.

Frank Mc Donald

The Greenhouse Effect

The Earth is warming; sinister and slow
The poisoned emanations waft above
Our all-protecting clouds, and we below
In fear and wonder for the Earth we love
Predict her woe.

The Earth is changing; once rich cornfields grew
Where now the desert spreads her sandy wings;
And barren hillsides that cannot renew
The verdure, crumble down to dried-up springs,
And no bird sings.

The Earth is striving, seeking to renew
Her freshness, but the follies of mankind
Still let the envenomed gases rise and spew
Into the skies, and no prevention find
Careless and blind.

The Earth is warming; harbingers and signs
Increase before the ever-watchful eyes
Of anxious men who question the designs
Of Time and Nature as the great seas rise
And cold declines.

The Earth is waiting; watching the icebergs melt
And waters drown the land beneath the surge
Of swirling waves. Cities where many dwelt
May be engulfed in the great ocean's verge
Never to emerge.

The Earth is dying; sonorous the sound
Of bells that echo through the deep seas surge: -
The peals of some cathedral long-since drowned
Echo mysterious though the waves submerge.
Shall this be her dirge?

Gay Ward

The Greenhouse Effect

'When icicles hang by the wall' . . .
Will future Eng Lit students know
The chilly grip of winter's thrall,
Or must dry footnotes stir recall
Of dictionary words like 'snow'?

Will 'winter of our discontent'
Be meaningless when January sun
Warms sprouting vines, when noon's in Kent
Are hotter than a Bedouin tent
in Wadi El-Haroun?

November's fogs, December's frost -
Will these be history? Will spring
And softer season's shapes be lost
As country saws and truths are crossed
And don't mean anything?

Ne'er cast a clout 'til May be out;
The lamb-and-lion moods of March;
Will April showers turn to drought,
Or Febr'ary Fill-dyke be in doubt
As Shrovetide sunshine's parch?

Constable's skies and Turner's rain,
Keat's Autumn, Wordsworth's daffodils,
Will be what duller dons explain,
No longer fresh; against the grain,
Just bookish memories, stills.

D A Prince

Overexposure

May-blossom froths in March, and daffodils
Droop prematurely withered yellow frills.
Like foolish, charmless drunks,
Robbed of all dignity, the gale-struck trees
Lean randomly; a mocking southern breeze
Plays gently round their trunks.

The climate's all awry: November storms,
A freakish January, stirring corms
And roots too soon to life,
A warm, dry, drought-inducing early Spring
That cracked the earth and shrivelled everything.
Now paranoia's rife:

Skin cancers will proliferate; around
The poles the ice will melt - we shall be drowned,
or frazzle anyhow;
Bright clouds of toxic gas will clog the sky;
The reservoirs and rivers will run dry . . .
We're all Cassandras now,

Except a fearless, fatalistic few
Who shrug and say there's nothing one can do
But revel in the heat:
Dig up that parched and wilting English rose,
Grow vines and figs on sun-drenched patios -
Turn Croydon into Crete!

Peter Norman

Twopence for a Shroud
A Hymn to the New World Order

We have built a new world order,
We are captains of our fate.
We have struck the high and mighty
And humbled his estate.
We can take the great decisions,
Who shall live and who shall die.
We are emperors of destiny,
Rulers of the sky.

When you hear that we are coming
You will know that help is nigh.
We will bomb your fields and factories
And teach you how to die.
We slaughter tens of thousands
And pile them heap on heap,
But we only count our own few dead
To prove that war is cheap.

Good citizens of Vietnam,
We helped you all we could.
We made the rain that burns the trees
To prove that God is good.
Good citizens of Panama,
'Tis true we sacked your town.
Your president was no true saint -
We swore to bring him down.

Good citizens of Lebanon,
Our ships they shelled your shore.
Just murmur freedom's sacred name
Then taste our guns once more.

Good citizens of Palestine,
Forget your own dear hills.
We hold you fast in servitude,
We feed the hand that kills.

Oh, mountaineers of Kurdistan,
Who took us at our word.
We urged you on to bloody war
To singe the tyrant's beard.
You raised the flag of liberty,
Your hearts beat true and proud.
You fought and froze and died alone -
Here's twopence for a shroud.

Good people of the wide, wide world,
Sleep peaceful, deep and still.
For deeper will they shortly sleep
Who thwart our iron will.
For in our new world order
'Tis we who make the choice.
We hold and love our own dear friends -
The others have no voice.

'To every man upon this earth
Death cometh soon or late.'
If others fall to prove our point
That price is not too great.
For justice is a noble ore,
We deal it by the ton.
Order reigns while infant bones
Lie scattered in the sun.

We have built a new world order,
We are captains of our fate.
We have struck the high and mighty
And humbled his estate.

Amid the devastation
We feel no pain nor gloom,
For we are lords of all the world -
Catalysts of doom.

M Maranka

The Friend

Now that the war of giants is safely fought,
One giant remains, who is our friend, though we
Must wonder whether this is what we sought.

With one so vast is friendship slavery?
Without some threat, can sweet acquaintance grow?
What is a friend without some enemy?

Though to the flights of memory I go
And fight again the battles that are gone,
The present always summons me to know

It is thin air our friendship flies upon
Such as one blundering act can dissipate.
A single barrel kills the flying swan,

Makes it warm stream of life coagulate
And turns it back to earth, from which it hails.
Precarious must be this friendship's state;

Yet it survives, and yet the white bird sails,
And still we hope for what the years may send,
Knowing that after all our logic fails.

Time stretches out towards no certain end.

Paul Griffin

Blank on the Map

How sad to think the sun would never set
On the blotched-red land we fought and held,
It worried me then - it worries me yet
That the bloodied sun would never meld
With the tired horizon and go down,
Peaceful, exhausted, quelled.

Why should the sun not sometimes shed his ray
Athwart and by-pass land where once it beat?
Yet still the Atlas voices have their say,
Still the trampling pilgrims tread their feet.
Red on the map! Why not (whisper) *blank?*
Empty, inclusive, sweet.

Eva Fitzpatrick

John Betjeman - a Tribute

Metroland! - the name is graven on a scroll that Time forgot;
Green and peaceful rural haven, quiet suburban Camelot.
Oh what resonance you carry, captured in the metric plan
Of that gentle visionary, prince of poets, Betjeman!

Join his train and take a journey on a well-upholstered seat,
Up to Harrow, Brill or Verney, outward bound from Baker Street.
Clerks ambitious, youths aspiring, making tracks for weekend fun,
Gaze with unassuaged desiring on the fair Miss Hunter Dunn.

See the farmland as it passes, interspersed with trim estates,
Mansions for the middle classes, upright husbands, houseproud
                                                                                  mates.
See the earnest parties hiking through the woodland greenery,
See the cyclists bravely biking, heartened by the thought of tea.

Yet great John's idyllic vision into nightmare is decayed,
Subject to the fierce elision of each change the world has made.
Litter and graffiti flourish; urban desecration fills
Run-down suburbs with its rubbish, Finchley Road to Northwood
                                                                                       Hills.

Double-glazing, blankly staring, framed in glossy PVC,
Vandalises, all uncaring, visual integrity.

Edward Welby

England Needs...

He loved the rhythms of the surf,
The sweep of sea-washed Cornish turf,
Here, the place that he loved best
He chose to take his final rest
Now time has closed that watchful eye
And laid the impish humour by,
On his grave the pygmies squat
And question, 'Was he a poet or not?'
Or should he be with scorn dismissed
As 'Just a lightweight satirist
Who peddled sentiment, and worse,
Made handsome profits from his verse,

A fellow who could 'turn a rhyme'
And 'hit the mark' from time to time,
Thus, phrase on trite pedestrian phrase
The critics damn with feeble praise,
Too overwhelmed in verbal dross
To comprehend our tragic loss,

In truth, the brightest light that shone
In Poetry's long dark night has gone,
The passion that restored the heart
To cerebral and loveless art,
The touch that gilds the commonplace
With qualities of style and grace,
The acid wit that savaged Slough
Come back, come back, we need you now.

Philip A Nicholson

Limerick

Though oft critical judgement diverges,
One name above others emerges:
  Erudite and well-read,
  And terrific in bed -
Yours faithfully, Anthony Burgess.

Colin Pearson

What is Housework

What is housework? Is it dusting
Corners that were not unclean,
Finding faults and imperfections,
Making changes and corrections,
Rubbing, scrubbing and adjusting?
Tell me, what does housework mean.

What is housework? Is it doing
Every day the same old chore?
Is it humble repetition
As a symbol of contrition,
Toiling, styling then reviewing?
Man was surely made for more.

What is housework? Is it knowing
Nothing mortal is complete?
When we think that we are winning
Back we go to the beginning,
Is it God's design for showing
Victory is slow defeat?

Or is housework resignation,
Doing things because we must?
Is it hope that someone sees us,
Call him Allah, Ra or Jesus,
Who to humour or to please us
Will reward our application,
And make diamonds out of dust?

Frank Mc Donald

Bird with Clipped Wings

One day I'll take the Golden Road. Today I can't go far;
Not Samarkand but Tesco is my goal.
One day, I'll seek the lost enchanted vale of Shangri-La
Or see the rose-red city . . . but I must bring in the coal.

One day, I'll soar the sunlit heights at forty thousand feet;
But for today the washing must be dried.
Potatoes wait for peeling and I have to mend that sheet
While in my mind the white sails fill to catch the evening tide.

One day, I'll have a ticket for the Orient Express
Or see historic castles of the Rhine;
But for today the iron is hot, a pile of shirts to press,
The windows all need cleaning and the furniture must shine.

Though longing still persists for magic places far away
Of mundane household products I must think,
Not sandalwood and spices from the shores of far Cathay.
I have to get a plunger and unblock the kitchen sink.

The meals to get and floors to mop and beds to make remain
While penguins walk across the Antarctic ice.
I'll never see the Taj Mahal or ride the wind to Spain.
One day, will I explore the dustless halls of Paradise?

Audrey Forbes-Handley

Prime Values

The swelling grapes are juicy on the vine,
The cheese is ripely ready and the wine,
Uncorked at last to let its subtle nose
Breathe on the air, vies with the full-blown rose.
The peach I pluck displays a perfect bloom,
Fine brandy mellows, and the spicy plume
Of lavender grows sweeter as it dries,
The grouse hang redolent, plump salmon rise.

Grained leather softens and old walnut glows,
New beauty in the muted hangings show,
That antique silver makes a rich display,
Old Masters grow in value every day.
Our fixed investments now have reached their term,
And blue-chip equities are holding firm.
As my endowment policy falls due
I'm getting out - all things mature but you!

Alanna Blake

Of Faith Maturing

There was a time I'd search for shooting stars
Hoping to find your footsteps in the dust
Of gentle Venus, Jupiter or Mars;
A time of soft hosannas, young in trust,
When words could heal and cynicism rang
Its leper's bell beyond my safe belief.
There was a time angels no longer sang
And I was bitter as the mocking thief,
When lost among the tombstones of the wise
I looked for famous names to canonise.

And I found no one. Forty summers stormed
The smug retreat where I sat obstinate;
I cast a glance on what I had deformed,
Wondering if my vision was too late.
But with that half-contrition all the dust
Of puzzled youth and immaturity
Became the substance of a second trust
Devoid of myth and empty sanctity.
I thought I'd lost your beatific view
Forgetting your boundless patience to pursue . . .

Frank Mc Donald

The Joys of Maturity

If you can watch the latest sexpot woo you
And stay unmoved by all the razzmatazz;
If you can greet the new religious guru
And scorn his ministry of jungle jazz;
If you can see those habits that annoy you
And feel no urge to kill but only kiss;
If you refuse to let your rage destroy you
When stung by meaningless atrocities;

If you can watch the young plunge into madness
Without becoming desperate or rude,
Viewing the melodrama not with sadness
But take a philosophic attitude;
If you accept you'll never lead the nation
Or leave a masterpiece that will endure
Though not perhaps a cause for jubilation
You may begin to think yourself mature.

Richard Blomfield

In Suspense

Held captive by the horny hands of heat
The lion drowses in the brittle grass.
A herd of wildebeest with weighted feet
Droops slowly forward in a languid mass
On sunbaked emptiness; the air, a sheet,
Shimmers and quivers round them like flawed glass.

A snaking gully in the mud long dried
Shows where last season's greedy river burst,
And salt-edged hollows in the distance hide
A bitter end for throats that burn with thirst.

A rash is itching red in neck and thighs,
Bellies are swollen; under wasting hair
Sharp sweat still trickles, blinding, into eyes
Which hold a blank acceptance in their stare,
Their listless lashes giving in to flies
That drink from tears a child can hardly spare.

Suddenly lightning cracks the swollen cloud
And lifts the waiting hills, the thunder key
Opens the burnt-out sky with rattles loud.
The air is light again, the rain falls free.

Alanna Blake

Merciful Release

Death could not last long enough for me:
Though Shakespeare prophesied a dateless night,
My sorrow seeks a new eternity
With darkness so inimical to light,
That galaxies of suns could not conspire
To permeate the all-pervasive gloom,
And Christ's whole heart, that flaming rose of fire,
Could not suffuse the darkness of the tomb.
And to that darkness I would add a chill,
A curling coldness that was so profound,
The deepest nerve of life would yet lie still,
However sweet the miracle it found,
And when Jehovah cried - 'Let there be light',
My soul would still be sealed in endless night.

Helen Forsyth

Hostage Crisis

They ushered him into the limelight,
Miming a message of hope;
Someone had thought it a time right
To untether the man from his rope.

He blundered his way through the pressmen
Who crowded around him at dawn;
To all these expressionless chessmen,
He was their prize of a pawn.

They'd fed him a diet of anguish,
Diatribe, darkness and pain;
Their language was letting his languish
Where silence became a refrain.

They offered him heartburn and headline,
They offered him flashbulb and cash,
But no-one had dealt with his deadline
And all were too brittle or brash.

He treated them hoarsely, with caution,
And parried their pressure, at peace;
Then he flew from their sport of distortion
To a distant, but blessed release.

Bill Greenwell

Sixteen or Natural Selection

Ahead of me the virgin soil of life,
Of love - vast territory to be explored -
And is my destiny to be a wife
Or one who is by countless men adored?
Restless within the confines of my bed,
I dream of sex and wonder will it be
An anticlimax, something I should dread,
Or sweet fulfilment of life's mystery?

Of such is the excitement of our youth.
Anticipation courses through our veins.
We travel hopefully and search for truth,
But nature needs to addle all our brains
So that we procreate; the human race
Abides - another generation wakes
And slides towards the sexual embrace.
This is the path all mortal flesh must take.

Maureen A Jeffs

Youth's Intensity

The joys of youth are largely over-rated:
Their energy, their hopes, their glowing skins,
Their chances, often unappreciated -
Such living standards! Such new-fangled sins!
By adults they're exhorted and berated
To use their gifts, to be the one who wins.

Oh yes, they have the world laid all before them,
And yes, they seem so blasé, so urbane;
And what to us were wonders simply bore them -
Yet I would not be seventeen again.
The media may flatter and adore them:
The only thing I envy is their pain.

After uncertain, callow adolescence,
The young acquire convictions firm and sure:
Their fury's fearsome in its incandescence;
They know despair and grief uniquely pure,
And pain of failed first love in its quintessence . . .
No wonder youth's a stuff will not endure.

The years will pass and blunt their sharper feelings,
And level out those breathless lows and highs;
Insentient scars accompany this healing
And balance is the consolation prize.
Life tempers youth with kindly Time's annealing,
But in the process, youth, unnoticed, dies.

Lindsay Staniforth

The Lost Battalion

I thought I saw in living truth
The lost battalion of my youth;
I told them all the news since they
Shouldered their arms and marched away,
Until with puzzled smiles they said:
'Who is the living? who the dead?'

I hear the lost battalion still,
Deep in the Burma of my will,
Dying to save me from defeat,
Fighting to cover my retreat,
Till I, without a deal of pain,
Stand in the line with them again.

Paul Griffin

Spring Laughter

You can hear it on the beaches, on the square and in the park,
You can recollect the pleasures of exploring in the dark,
You may wish to close your ears to it, and write it off as dead
But your dreaming damns your reasoning, and spring is in your head.

Though the laughter that accompanies the games you cannot share
Is the laughter of the esplanade, when all the beach is bare,
To hell with old sobriety your lips appear to say,
Your heart admits no breathlessness, nor has your hair turned grey.

You are younger than the youngest if you strike that perfect note
That makes a commonplace celestial and lets your feelings float
To a high point in a heaven where the month is always May
And the blossoming of promises will never fade away.

Ah, but wait a moment longer for the trumpet call of truth
That admits no old impostors to the palaces of youth,
Can it be those bursts of laughter that you thought were so sublime
Were the railings of a scornful world, and mockeries of time?

Frank Mc Donald

Youth

The aged in the throes of thought
At how their years have come to nought
Persist in harping on the joy
Of when they were a 'girl' or 'boy'.

But no-one thinks they're young when young
Unless they're dull or highly-strung:
The joy of youth, if truth be told,
Is thinking that you're really old.

A sense of your mortality
Is, when you're barely twenty-three,
Quite honestly what pleasure means -
A proof that you've escaped your teens.

The past (in rompers) lends its zest
To youth. Ahead lies Thirty, dressed
For surgery in dirty gown:
Youth's halfway-up, not halfway-down.

And as for sex or spice or speed,
Irreverence of sporting deed -
These are the froth, the anyhow;
The joy of youth is always Now.

Bill Greenwell

The Joy of Sex

From a rolling in the clover on a perfect summer day
To a snuggle in the duvet in the cold of winter grey,
Though some think it is pernicious,
There is nothing more delicious
Than a sexual encounter, and the game that adults play.

It's a warming of the cockles, and a heating of the brain
It's the exercise that benefits and leaves no trace of pain,
And no matter what the fashion
Of fulfilment of your passion,
There's nothing else quite like it for relieving mental strain.

Oh, the closeness and the softness of a partner's naked flesh,
Oh, the unity of spirit as the lovers' parts enmesh
Oh the heartbeats loudly racing
To the rhythm of embracing,
As the world explodes and paradise is reconceived, afresh.

Katie Mallett

The Lovely Trains

And then there are the trains, the lovely trains,
Racing through the nights, racing through the days,
Cutting through snowdrifts, through industrial haze,
Through Southern sunlight, and through North Sea rains:
The trains that chugged and steamed through childhood dreams;
The trains of close encounters - O that gaze -
Newfangled trains tracked on computer screens -
What bliss to watch in frame on frame appear
The vineyards, orchards, cities of romance;
To walk from underground to sunlit square
Still dreaming in some medieval trance -
Then wake next morning in the different air
Of Prague or London, Venice or Provence.

Robert Perry

DSS Welcome

The Hotel Grand in Paddington
Is dirty, cold and bleak
And men live there in dormitories
For forty quid a week.

Under a stuccoed ceiling rose
Six to a room they lie
Their hands are lax and on their backs,
They rest without a sigh.

The cellar kitchen fills with smoke,
They cook their own hot meals,
The food comes down in plastic bags
Since everybody steals.

They watch the telly while they eat,
It drowns both thought and speech;
A man in leather clothes emits
A schizophrenic screech.

Eleven, twelve, they still arrive,
A sad and blackfaced crew
Of broken, workless, hopeless men
With tubes of special brew.

Sleep comes to one and all at last
As death must come one day
And in the stench a fire glows
To keep the frost away
And one calls out, a muffled shout
'Hepl me, my God, I pray!'

The Hotel Grand in Paddington
Is dirty, chill and bleak
And men of every age find there
The comforts that they seek.

Austin Johnson

Always With

The poor are always with us, see the hands
Outstretched for aid, the guilt-provoking eyes,
The bubble bellies, as on burning sands
The sick are made obscene by crawling flies.

We send them food and clothes, we dig some wells,
The wherewithal to grow a decent crop,
And pray, as pity for the children swells,
That famine and its suffering will stop.

But, the poor are always with us, see the gaunt
And joyless faces in the orphanage
In eastern Europe. As their faces haunt
Our sleepless nights, we seethed with silent rage.

We bring them from their hell into our heaven
Of consumerism, never mind the cost.
As if each Barbie Doll or teddy given
Could bring them back the childhood they have lost.

The poor are always with us, see the rags
On waste tip scavengers, the worn and cold
With all they have in crumpled dustbin bags,
The cardboard city dwellers, young and old.

We give them soup, and blankets for their backs,
A shelter maybe, a degree of pride,
We think maybe the rich should pay more tax
To keep them off the streets and riverside.

The poor are always with us, see the look
Of deprivation in a youngster's face,
He hasn't a computer, though a book
Would teach him more, he wallows in disgrace.

His trainers aren't in fashion, and his room
Does not contain a video machine.
His peers' derision fuels his growing gloom,
His sense of poverty is real and keen.

The poor are always with us. Although thirst
And hunger may be finally consigned
To history, still someone will feel cursed -
Poverty not gone, but redefined.

Katie Mallett

Fortune and Men's Eyes

They lie in cardboard boxes there
And wait for light and luck to come.
But what they do is their affair,

They've lost their roots and are aware
They are the sick, the drunk, the scum.
They lie in cardboard boxes there.

Some broken men are in despair
And feel they earn opprobium.
But what they do is their affair.

Sad, homeless youths and girls just stare,
Unwanted, from each pavement slum.
They lie in cardboard boxes there.

Some beg and whine, some spit and swear.
They're hungry, cold and troublesome.
But what they do is their affair.

The wheel of fortune spins its share
Of want and poverty to some.
They lie in cardboard boxes there.
But what they do is their affair.

Jenny Morris

Rich or Poor

A guileless curate cycles in the rain,
His life is simple, self-denying, plain,
For cakes and ale don't rule out bread and wine,
To crave is human, to forgo, divine.

The rain falls also on a sullen youth,
(His appetites are all he knows of truth);
To duties blind, insistent on his rights,
The hand that feeds him is the hand he bites.

These two are equals in financial worth,
But one sees life's abundance, one its dearth,
For values make us rich or make us poor -
Such poverty's not cured by having more.

Tim Hopkins

Soup Kitchen

Don't nail with that bloody gaze,
Bring up with that accusing cough
The desolation of your days,
This hook you never let me off.

Stand back. I cannot bear the scratch
Of stubble on your cheek's grey plain,
Lit by the trembling of a match,
A glowing butt you suck again

Through mittened finger, calloused thumb,
To fire the dissipated meths
That make your lonely hours less numb,
Add vigour to those rasping breaths.

Take your protection for the night:
Newspaper blankets, plastic socks.
Drag all your problems out of sight
And mind, inside your cardboard box.

Round scattered crumbs and empty urn
A warmth pervades the moving van.
As charity strikes chill, we turn
From man's inhumanity to man.

Alanna Blake

In the Supermarket

In infinite small choices, trapped
By long neglect and shrivelling age,
She puzzles 'Special Offers', wrapped
In threadbare coat and muffled rage.

Where money matters choice comes down
To matching small coins in her purse;
All finer tastes are left to drown.
Not what is better, what is worse

But what is cheap and what will fill,
Until next pension day comes round.
The pennies counted at the till,
The tireless stretching of each pound

Keep her alive. Her voice is thin;
Her eyes, blanked with sour want, are pale
Each movement's costed. Nameless in
The shuffling crowd, brittle and frail,

She dreads the gnaw of winter's cold,
Living as much as dying, days
Greyer than fog, and being old,
And poverty's claw-fingered ways.

D A Prince

Alan Coren

The profundities of Shakespeare,
Thomas Hardy's tragic themes,
The wit of J K Jerome,
H G Wells' prophetic dreams,

Merit lasting fame and glory
But for me the wit and style
Of this Perelman disciple
Eternally beguile.
Contemporary trivia
Fuels the fire of Coren's Muse,
Overheard pomposity's,
Strange odds and ends of news,
The visible absurdities
That governments create,
The self-inflatory antics
Of the temporary 'Great'
In what he calls his feuilletons
He brilliantly displays
His magic power to deftly twist
The tired familiar phrase;
No nuances of common speech
Escape his perfect ear,
Twixt earthy slang and scholarship
His wicked fancies veer -

This man who uses flippancy
As others use a sword
Must surely when the wise ones meet
Receive his just reward,
Indeed it's said that in those haunts
Of literary rumour,
Low urgent whispers grow apace,
'Alan Coren - Humour!'

Philip A Nicholson

To Henry Vaughan, Who Needs no Praise

I visited your grave the other day,
Behind the church, above the Usk;
Three centuries of quiet decay
Have come and gone, with dawn and dusk.
What we decide to value too
Has altered, like your reputation:
The Silurist, we now hold you
An honoured poet of your nation.

But you, if with us nowadays,
Might well reflect that an OM's
For meditation: God's the praise,
No order or merit else in poems.
For 'honours' must to you seem slight,
Who saw Eternity one night.

Don Rodgers

In Honour . . . Philip Bourke-Marston

Philip Bourke-Marston lived and died
More than a hundred years ago -
His books of sonnets, called *Songtide,*
Quite touched my heart; he longed to know
If someone, someday, on Life's Shore,
Would hear his Songtide echoing . . .
I hear it now - its essence more
The poignant, for Time's harrowing . . .
Dear Poet, blind and dispossessed
Of love - your birthright's legacy -
I hear your Songtide now - expressed
In words, etched in my memory . . .

And if there is a Hall of Fame,
In golden letters, ten feet high,
Upon the wall, I'll write your name -
So you will know that, such as I,
Through all the joys and tears Life brought -
Have kept the faith your love impressed . . .
Dear Philip Marston, you have caught
And struck a chord, deep in my breast . . .
Dear Archetype and Poet's light,
The Dreamer in the Visionary -
Your Songtide echoes, day and night -
A heartbeat - for eternity!

C F Marfell-Harris

Hell

Hel our mother brought us forth,
Her red blood renews the earth;
From her breasts of smoke and snow
Unimagined beauties grow.

At her sacred nether gate
Souls re-enter human fate.
Word reviled by ingrate men!
Blaze its holiness again!

Helen, Ellen, Cinderella,
Remembered by the storyteller,
How shall we restore you, now
Slavery's stamped upon your brow?

In catastrophic nuptial heat
Our elements were forged complete;
Lover her savage wisdom, tell,
Reverentially, of 'elle'.

Elizabeth Imlay

Kenealy's Version

It was Kenealy told me about Hell.
I'd heard of it, of course, but in my thin,
Grey nonconformist world, we used to swell
More on the demon drink, or on the sin
Of Sabbath laughter. But Kenealy, now,
Had got it from the Fathers, who could set
The scene with relish, trace each anguished brow,
Zoom in on every contrite bead of sweat.

Kenealy - who was twelve or so, and had
A wicked line in leg-breaks - told me all:
The tearing flames, the boils that drove you mad,
The gagging thirst with no relief but gall;
Your flesh commingling with the putrid throng;
The stench, the rending din; no light, no friend.
And, worst, the knowledge that, however long
You suffered, there was more. No term, no end.

I tried to put him straight (I was a year
His senior). I told him firmly how
Fallacious were these fleshly baits for fear:
Scare tactics, cunningly designed to cow
The simple to obedience. Even so,
Sometimes a doubt comes creeping in the night:
Since there's so little we can truly know,
I wonder, could Kenealy have been right?

Noel Petty

Hell, a New Eternity

(With apologies to J M)

Satan and his cronies are preparing for the fray
As election time in hell is looming closer every day.
Infernal airwaves crackle with vituperous debates,
Sin and Death distribute leaflets to the sinners at the gates.

Ten thousand demon activists form factions left and right
And broadcast manifestos through eternities of night.
The sons of Belial clamour for more sulphur in the air
While Abdiel leads the Snot-Greens to defend the brimstone layer.

Beelzebub the Militant builds bonfires in the gorge,
Incinerating Charters which the Satanists have forged.
Grim Satan spins the calendar and plays about with dates
While all his loyal demons bribe the Furies and the Fates.

In hell's darkness no one notices the ceasing of the days,
And Satan only chuckles at his dev'lish clever ways:
Election fever burns perpetual, yet the day will never come,
So the Prince of Darkness triumphs and his course is never run.

Katherine Turner

A Glimpse Beyond the Veil

I heard the organ's plaintive swell
And thus, I thought, the angels sang;
I heard His hymns, I knew them well
And held my breath when servers rang
The transubstantiation bell.

With pious hands I made my prayer
'I am not worthy, Lord, to come,'
I felt that incense in the air
And rays from the ciborium
Could penetrate a childish stare.

At times when warming Christmas snow
Fell on illuminated glass,
God was a sanctuary glow,
A sleepy voice at midnight mass,
That summoned shepherds long ago.

Now they have closed that sacred veil
And darkness meets and old man's eyes,
God's little artifices fail
To succour, frighten or surprise.

There are no roads that lead again
To little churches, snug as prayer,
No requiems to heal the pain
Of disillusion and despair.

But sometimes, sometimes when the sun
Pretends to be as bright as God,
An old man dallies, just for fun,
With past religion's fire and fraud,
Letting Him think that He has won.

Of course the old man knows too well
That bread is bread and wine is wine,
That childhood eyes could never tell
Man's cleverness from the divine,
Or bluff from consecration bell.

But ask him, on a winter's day,
Of cities built upon a hill,
Of mustard seed, or Passion Play,
Ask, and he shall remember still,
For some things never pass away.

Frank Mc Donald

To a Beloved Robin

A dismal day and I am gloomy too:
The rhythm, words and metre - are all wrong;
But there you are arriving right on cue
To warm my wintry heart with summer song.
To sit serenely in my favourite tree -
Your red breast ruffled by a bitter blast -
And sing to me of life that is to be,
Of glory which will never be surpassed.
The beauty of your music fills the air
And all around reflects your fervent praise;
You are a living answer to my prayer,
A harbinger of hope on cloudy days.
Time after time God shows me He is near
And of His creation I revere.

Maureen Jeffs

The Shaft of Light

How can *true* knowledge fade and disappear?
Where does it go? Only the other day
My fingers touched the stars, and yet today
Known formulations blur, to reappear
As dusty platitudes at which to peer
Uncomprehendingly. It slipped away -
My recognition of the gods at play,
The Shaft of Light that showed me why I'm here . . .
But has it really gone, or does it lie
Below the surface of the clouded mind -
A reservoir of truth whose rich supply
Can never be depleted by mankind.
Light will not fail, but we who occupy
The *other* end of heaven can be blind . . .

Stella Browning

And Let the Credit go

Paradise to come does not
Engage my interest one jot.
What makes my vital juices flow
Are minor pleasures here below,
The cut and thrust of hard-fought chess,
Bridge games of infinite finesse,
Good conversation, books, fine wine
Eccentric humour matching mine -
Small concerns in which I find
Rich food for body, soul and mind
Fine fare which gives me as I feed
All the heaven that I need
Content - perhaps too soon - with this
I waive all claims to future bliss.

Philip A Nicholson

To my Wife

If I have sought the depth of love to tell,
'Twas not false pride in my unworthy tongue
That bade me sing the songs left long unsung;
Nor thought I that my voice could tune them well.

No words that yet were fashioned could explain
The nature of my love, nor set its bound;
What can I say? Since language has no sound
To compass love, my own weak voice is vain.

Unbounded as the universe above,
So is the strength and passion of that grace
That binds me as thy slave; nor seeks to rove
In search of further beauty. Could you trace
The Paths Eternal, you should find my love
Beyond all light and thought, all time and space.

Allan Warbis

A Literate Love

I trawled the Celtic twilight,
A child of Innisfree,
Who longed to fly with linnet's wings
And hear the honey bee.

I followed you in youth again
For I discovered more,
Your armours and your tragedies,
Your tales of grief and war,

But, raven hair and floppy tied,
A goose became a swan
And Willy played a Jupiter
Whose Leda was Maud Gonne.

I looked for you in Dublin,
At Coole and Ballylee.
Alone I climbed the winding stair
For none was there for me.

I journeyed to Byzantium,
I sought you in Japan
And searched among the Samurai,
A brokenhearted fan.

I studied cones and spirals
That I might plumb your soul
And make a psychic marriage
With a spiritual goal.

Let philistines neglect you,
But I'll remain the fool
Who hopes to resurrect you
At the Yeats soc Summer School.

Patricia V Dawson

To my (School) Mistress

Like some awed pupil I await your call;
Attentively, a thousand times I stare
At the degrees of beauty that you wear,
Gowned in the lights that on your shoulders fall.
The textbooks of your body tells me all;
I find all subjects and all lessons there,
A syllabus of love beyond compare;
And it alone is educational.

It must be so, for I am daily turning
Wiser from all my studies at your will.
Though men may say such tutelage at best's
A supplement to life, my life's in learning
That secret knowledge born of lying still
In the enchanted classroom of your breasts.

Paul Griffin

Stigmata

Over twenty years ago
When we came to meet,
I was searching, half a pair.
You were one, complete.

I did not stretch out my hand,
Did not risk rebuff.
You, who are a mind on legs,
Don't need a touch enough.

I paired off and you did not,
Welcome single guest.
Chat and smile, but long to be
Curled against your breast.

Just three times in half my life
I have felt your hand
Scarcely brush my wrist or flank
Life a waft of sand.

Slightest contact, greatest shock -
Scorched my singing flesh.
Three clear outlines of your hand
Tingle now, still fresh.

Down the lonely married years,
Loved but not caressed,
How I treasured these three prints
Carelessly impressed.

Helen Chown

To X

I could fall in love with you my mild old friend.
You were always like a house half-glimpsed around a bend.
After twenty years is it too late?
You offered me yourself once on a plate.
I turned it down with many a mystic flourish:
'I love another madly.' You said, 'Rubbish,
Take the offered Good; don't act so young.'
For Age read Decadence thought I, much stung.
Would you take me now with half peeled Youth?
Or am I just a dear old pal
(Your burning love, your pillar of fire,
Windswept, naked, with no shame,
A paradise that never goes,
Your ultimate arrival in the rose)
Tell me (can I hear the news?) the truth.

Jill Neville

A Good Death

How can we call Death good - the foe to life?
Yet poets say he brings men longed-for ease,
Rest after toil, peace after long-drawn strife,
Port after stormy seas.

Old, now, and sometimes weary, still I cling
To mortal life, well loved because well known,
And dread the hour set for my journeying
Into the dark alone.

And envy my dead friends their Christian faith
Who on the strength of Holy Church relied,
And, helped by rites and prayers, embraced their death
Prepared and fortified.

O that my faith were stronger, courage more!
I look about for comfort, and I think
Of Bunyan's pilgrims as they reach the shore
And stand upon the brink.

Standfast, whose marks and scars proclaim his zeal,
Undaunted braves the dreadful river's tide,
And wins across, and for him trumpets peal
Upon the other side.

And that faint-hearted pilgrim, *Much-Afraid,*
Who so dreads death, to things familiar clinging,
Reaches the waterside, poor, timid maid,
And then - goes over singing!

Some suffer violent deaths; others more mild:
Martyrs and heroes, Spartans on their shields,
And that old sinner, Falstaff, like a child,
Babbling of green fields.

Were these Good Deaths? Courage is good, and faith,
But what of Death, the Arch-Foe at the end?
Saint Francis greets him as our Brother Death
And says he comes as friend.

Few, surely, long to exceed their mortal span.
Birth, growth, and then decay . . . Is that the whole?
And not unwelcome comes the call to man:
Go forth, O Christian soul!

Myfanwy Lloyd

A Good End

I turned and looked at something else instead
In war, when dying stared me in the face;
But afterwards, thoughts fluttered in my head.

Winged contemplation feeds on time and space,
Which clarify the brain; when time is short,
Off fly our judgements of the human case.

Now, in old age, all has to be re-fought;
I see no time remains, in panic see
The end of breath, the end of time for thought,

And once again look round in misery
For something else to dwell on, hoping so
To drive away the dreaded enemy.

Here in the regiment of age of go
And live again the battles that were gone.
Why should I need to think? I cannot know

What journey death is going to launch me on.
It is an instant's agony to part.
Can it be good, this dreaded Dies Non

That checks the panic thunder of the heart?

Paul Griffin

Good Death

The day is going, turmoil's cease,
Across the hill the gentle shadows softly lie.
So may a calm and restful peace
Enfold us when we die.
No more to strive, no more to grieve,
No more to fret or trouble those we leave,
But let the tired eyelid close
Over the tired eye.
Good deeds we will have done in life and ill:
Softly the shadows lie across the hill.

Charles Porter

Death of Deaths

The martyr died sustained by faith,
The soldier by his creed,
The plunderer in the frenzy
And the fury of his greed,

The celebrity made quittance
Amid honour and acclaim,
Hopes, ambitions, realised,
Cocooned in earthly fame,

The sick man bore long illnesses
Resolutely, strove to face
His lingering extinction
With fortitude and grace,

The suicide went from us
In the grip of dark despair
And the shattering confusion,
Of a mind beyond repair;

Some of these died well enough
For each in his own way
Had weighed the cost of living
And knew the price to pay,

But all good deaths are fathered by
That one upon the cross,
The ultimate exemplar
Of redemption found through loss,

A death at which I marvel still,
How could such wonder be,
To sacrifice so much to give
Eternal life to me?

Philip A Nicholson

Mercy

I tipped the capsules down the kitchen sink -
They had no power to dull the knives of pain.
I poured the four-star cognac out to drink,
Brimming the cut-glass snifter; then the strain,

Ensuring the decision now was right:
A Haydn mass, the final songs of Strauss?
The changing into something warm and light,
A last brisk look around the emptied house.

I fetched the plastic bag: unerring this,
When it was fitted and securely tied;
I drew my courage from that final kiss
And knelt, and held her hands until she died.

Alanna Blake

A Good Death

Clearing old clothes, the one suit hardly worn,
She thought 'He made a good death' 'though not sure
How, what she meant, other than shabby, poor
Grey-faced and stooping, chill in his final dawn
She'd found him, in the room where he was born,
No longer struggling bravely to endure
His scraped-together shards of life, obscure
But decent, caught on poverty's thorn.
Once over, death made no demands, nor could -
Freed from indignity, beyond all speech -
Still cling with desperate hands to those who tend
The friendless - social workers, doctors - each
Milestones to some long-sought release, an end
Not troubling others: all we now call good.

D A Prince

Terror

Four horsemen with blank faces, spurring down
A slope I seem to know, above the town,
Brandishing swords - the moonlight sees the glint
Of sharpened steel. I turn my heart to flint
Death being certain as each thudding steed
Carrying an eyeless devil, blind as Fate
Drawn down toward me by some bloody hate,
Rides quickly on: is this some cruel joke,
Or, if I feel that first and fatal stroke
Before I wake, shall I be dead indeed?

Moment of terror: I begin to scream,
But no sound comes to wake me from my dream . . .

Richard Graves

After Death

Night always was your time. Loving was best
After the trees dissolved, and when the sky
Drank colour from the darkening garden. Rest
You never needed, nor were nourished by

Rich silences, or pauses for repose.
So are you now. I could have wished you
Stiller, or sadder, half-remembering those
Long pleasures we enjoyed before I knew

Death, and its aching cold. If you should feel
An unexpected chill in July's heat,
Or see the swallows in unnatural wheel
Or fear more bitter sting in winter's sleet

Do not dismiss as wild imaginings
My only way to reach you after death,
And, turning to your newer love's beginnings,
Laugh these faint doubts away - a waste of breath

To acknowledge all we used to share,
Or that too soon you ceased to mourn and grieve.
Night's eyes and mine grow paler. In despair
The trees take shape. Silent, I take my leave.

D A Prince

Doppelganger

The ghost of who I might have been,
Kneels wordless by my bed,
The spectre of a better man,
Whose life I could have led.

He holds a volume locked and chained,
Whose story would be mine,
If love had been my wafered bread,
And truth my altar wine.

O vanity of vanities,
Hope's crucible grows cold,
God's alchemy alone transmutes
Base metal into gold.

Tim Hopkins

House of the Dead

The briefcase in the hall, black coat
spread-eagled on the banister. The clocks
tick through the dead hours of the night
an unaccustomed solitude. The books,

stranded on the dusty shelves, lie there
like wasted opportunities. I'd sit, drink, dream
a self which trembles on the outer stair
now looking in. There is a motto theme

persists through life: the stacked cassettes,
CD's in silence mock an inattention.
What I remember is my talent to forget.
Inheritor of premature distinctions,

young savage in the drawing-room, and once
Hegel in Hertfordshire amongst spittoons
in boom-time, I'm a listener now to clocks
and heartbeats, all the liberties I took

dissolved in stale cigar-smoke. Much too late
the night lays claims. The child's room
is empty, and the double-bedroom not too great
to case an inchoate spirit in, become

one fearing daybreak, one which best may hope
a spectral stranger will descend the staircase,
don the old black overcoat, take briefcase up
in grip of a sepulchral hand, release

the lock's reverberating music, leave the house
to all the others who may come to haunt it,
though unnoticed, once the gate's click knows
that he who closes it will not revisit.

And the house will then turn in on itself,
absorbed, and clocks fall silent, and the dust
drop silent through the silent rooms, enough,
particle on particle alike, to then suggest

beyond a human case, or curse, or brief caress,
time's grand unhuman regal carelessness.

Roger Caldwell

Déjà-Vu

The church lies sunken deep in grass
long summer hours the shadows pass
and scatter threads of holy light
reflected in the broken glass;

in summer drowse or winter night
eerie at twilight and at night
holy and hushed and evermore
as caught in some Enchanter's flight.

O sacred spell from days of yore
alone I dwelt here long before:
I am the Spirit of the place,
I linger here and I adore

each crooked patch upon the floor,
the moss grown on the half-hinged door,
the marble sunk, the dusty tomb,
the rusty iron, the laden gloom.

I am the Ghost whose grief and grace
sustain the still of slanting noon
lest men return again and soon
wound womb and orb of silence, chase

each holy thing away and slake
their lust to break and bruise, and shake
the intricacies spider weaves
in tangled parables of leaves,

ravage the sacred as they make
my Father's house a den of thieves.

Elizabeth Sadik

Commuter Train

Near Cricklewood, where the joined houses show
Their shabby backs to railway lines below,
A glance while slowing down before the station
Revealed a most unusual situation.

A naked youth stood in a window bay,
Not facing me, but turned the other way.
Although the glimpse was momentary and slight
It filled me with a wondering delight.

Was he an exhibitionist poseur
Catering for the travelling voyeur?
Or posing for a class, or simply dressing?
Conjecture crumbled into idle guessing.

Monotonous commuting takes me past
The terraced houses, all from first to last
The same. But never have I seen again
The vision of that beautiful young man.

Barbara Balch

First Sighting

Carrying a bunch of early daffodils
I went to Hampstead, in a lazy train
To see my aunt in the Royal Free again
Who'd overdosed on some quick-slimming pills.

And while my train was stalled at Willesden station
I glanced into another - going west -
And saw the object of a whole life's quest,
A girl who beggared my imagination.

Her eyes met mine, I swear I saw her start,
She blushed, but still she didn't look away,
I tried to guess the train's projected stay
To calculate how soon it might depart.

I knew - I simply knew that I must act!
How far away, and how steep were the stairs?
One of Eternity's predestined pairs
Had glimpsed each other in the world's wide tract

But parted by two sealed, thick panes of glass,
Prisoners in trains conspiring to diverge
At any time. In a tormented surge
Of love I held the flower up, gold as brass,

Held out my arms; smiled; begged her with my eyes
And she, one finger slender as a taper
Held to her lips, hushed me, then found a paper
And quickly wrote - but what I daren't surmise,

Her name? Her stop? Her number or address,
A message - surely positive and kind!
But my train jerked and she was left behind
Before I had the chance to mime distress.

Too late I realised what I should have done,
Then fretted; got out, followed, far too late,
Questioned the bored collector on the gate
Of every station, working down the run.

But when I reached the end not one recalled
And angel with green eyes and white dress.
Her long fair hair had quite failed to impress
These dismal louts and I was left stone-walled.

Dispirited, exhausted, cursed and shoved
I staggered out towards the telephone
To make excuses to poor auntie Joan,
And saw there, boxed in light, the one I loved.

Mortimer Spreader

To Annabel

You passed me in the office, and I could not help but stare
At the sinuous oscillations of your charming derrière.
You turned and help me spellbound with your fascinating gaze -
In an instant I was smitten and our passion was ablaze.

Like two meteors in orbit that engage in outer space,
Like the confluence of rivers, like the sacrament of grace,
Like the melding of two shadows in the blinding midday sun,
We two that had been strangers were ecstatically one.

Who can pen the wild explosion that assails the mental state
When the hormones set in motion the compulsive urge to mate?
Within days we conjugated in a bout (the first of many)
On a luxury four-poster in a hotel in Kilkenny.

Oh the sweet intoxication of those silken nippled moons!
What delightful penetration, what sublime orgasmic swoons!
Irresistibly we bonded, which inevitably led
To a day when we absconded, and another when we wed.

But the surging tides of passion were in matrimony curbed,
And the wailing plaints of infants were our nights of love disturbed,
And the furrowed brow of labour and the anxious quest for gold
Preoccupied our psyches - until suddenly we're old!

Now the fledglings have departed and again we are but two,
And amazingly, we're started an adventure all anew.
For machinery grown rusty once again begins to turn,
And the embers of the furnace rediscover how to burn.

Though we cannot now recapture that pervasive early force,
The unbounded flood of rapture which propelled us on our course,
We know that (given patience) we can celebrate with pride
The latter-day renaissance of love that never died.

Edward Welby

The New Neighbour

The winter rose stood frozen, dead,
Still waiting for the sun to glow;
The crocus raised its purple head
And melted through a ring of snow.

Your spade's cold blade was scraping back
Our common path, you broke away
The ice: I heard the water crack
And glisten in the rising day.

The garden crunched beneath your feet:
The brittle leaves; the hoary grass.
I waited for our eyes to meet,
We smiled across the frosty glass.

I shivered as you asked my name;
We shared a brew to pass the day.
Cold loneliness until you came
To brush the frozen dust away.

G R Harvey

Food, Glorious Food

Food is God's weapon. When I was expelled
From Eden, great hard hands, red-rubber-gloved,
Suspended me in air. All that I loved
And thought so permanent was lost. I yelled
For my return to un-life, and was held
In new, rough comfort. Firm upon my tongue,
A solid softness pushed, and in my young
Distress, I sucked, and found my protest quelled.
And so, reluctantly, I lived for food,
And started to enjoy the waking dream
Provoked by Eden's apple. (Served with cream
When softly baked is best, but also good
In fluffy piles on pork.) With fork and knife
I celebrate the helplessness of life.

Alison Prince

Plea Bargain

Lord deprive me if you must
Of money, power and fame,
Filch form me ambition, lust,
Honour and good name,

Desert me at the end, cast down,
Dishonoured and debased,
But spare me, when you've had your fun,
The cruel theft of taste,

For even when alone, bereft
Of hearing, sense, and sight,
I'd not complain if I was left
The boon of appetite,

Small hardship for me then, the pain
Of sad decrepitude
If to the last I could retain
My lifetime love of food.

Philip A Nicholson

A Russian Poet Laments His Freedom

When revolutionaries celebrate
The downfall of a village or a state,
They hold their automatic weapons high,
One-handed (for they too have seen John Wayne)
And rattle off their volleys to the sky.
Bullets, to them, come cheaper than champagne.

I did the same; I, who in the attic cell
Had hoarded words, sworn to make each one tell.
A sniper's discipline. But from that store
Light-headed, I released my sharp-nosed words,
As though they had no value any more.
They soared awhile, then vanished, wild as birds.

Now no one cares. Perhaps I should have let
My head appear above the parapet.
Then, in some gulag, kept by stone-faced brutes,
Using grey paper and a smuggled pen,
What poems might have lined my rotting boots?
Freedom's cold meat. I will not write again.

Noel Petty

Togrop

You gave me the wing of the morning,
A shield and a sword for my soul,
A flame for my spirit's adorning,
A pillar of fire for my goal.

You gave me a knowledge of beauty,
A judgement of good and of ill;
You gave me a task and a duty;
You gave me a mind and a will.

You gave me a world full of laughter,
The love of a partner and friend,
The promise of glory hereafter,
And wisdom and truth in the end.

You gave me Your sons and Your daughters.
'All these are your brethren,' You said.
Now hide me, O God, for the waters
Of life are come over my head.

Allan Warbis

Life's Persecution

In a little while frost will find the flower
I cultivate with something less than pride,
and I'll shiver in the absence of a sun
that watches the wind take everything I tried
to clothe in meaning. In a little while
these fingers that obey a call to write
will stiffen in a colder, kinder soil,
as Time seeks out another acolyte.
In a little while this soft insanity
of breathing just to breathe will pass away
and then the mind will grow alert and know
which thoughts to leave aside, which prayers to pray . . .
as though it mattered. In a little while
strangers will drink my cup, and those I love
will fill their thoughts with mine and all but touch
these last remaining moments when I move
from death to death, from nothing back to dust.

Frank Mc Donald

With Wild Flowers For my Father's Grave

Sleep on, in Dalnawillan's earth secure.
What if these flowers fade? Their roots endure.

Angus Sinclair

Family Albums

In smiling immobility
Or frenetically at play,
Behold the ideal family
In polychrome array;
Giggled over, gloated on,
Extravagantly praised,
Arcadian domesticity
Presented matt or glazed,
Frozen in a world where all
Is harmony and light,
An Eden of tranquillity
With not a snake in sight -

Ah, but there's another album
(Photographer unknown),
Secreted in the attic
Sometimes seen but never shown,
Images of discontent
In grainy black and grey,
Featuring our little group
In quite a different way.
Gone the easy bonhomie
The 'ear to ear' grimace,
Atop each pair of shoulders sits
A 'Spitting Image' face,

A face that outwardly reflects
The turbulence within,
As the serpent of dissension
Lisps his litany of sin:

Philip A Nicholson

The Widow's Table

Unthinking, from old habits, she sets out
three places at the table - then,
catching herself in this untimely act,
sighs that old days can't return again.

I turn aside my face, I've had enough
of moistened eyes and, if the truth be said,
am all too eager to live out my youth
amongst my kind and not amongst the dead.

I, only son, will leave as soon as I am able,
now certificates are signed and duties done.
Tonight there are two places at the table.
Tomorrow she will need to lay but one.

Roger Caldwell

In Memoriam

God is in his heaven,
the devil lives in hell.
I live at number seven,
me Daddy does as well.

Me Daddy's name if Terry,
he can sing and he can fight.
He's the toughest man in Derry,
but he sometimes cries at night.

Ain't seen me Mam for ages,
she don't live here no more.
Me prayer book's lost two pages,
Dad threw it on the floor.

I got a friend called Pammy,
she said me Mammy's dead.
The Cathlics killed me Mammy,
least that's what Pamla said.

She said me Dad's a Proddy,
Mam shunta married him.
That's why they smashed her body,
and dumped it in a bin.

Me Daddy hates all Cathlics,
he said so on TV.
I'm a little Cathlic,
I hope he don't hate me.

Richard Charles

Mens Insana

You thought you had the answer
A test tube full of genes,
Some fruit flies in a glass jar
Plus quick mutating beans.

You thought that if you sliced up
Some monkey meat quite fine,
And poked and peered and prodded
You'd find the human line.

You thought - you didn't think friends,
You've fallen off the rails,
You cannot find the answer
Within your own entrails.

And then with Mathematica
And telescopes in air
You squinted at the heavens
Shouted 'Answer if you're there'

Equations cannot formulate
The shape and size of souls,
You haven't learned to listen
So you've only found black holes.

H St G Cramp

Foolishness With God

In our summer we had heaven and we mocked His revelations
We were trendy existentialists, rejecting preparations
For a wintertime of weeping, full of judgements and repentance,
We had atheistic wisdom and our jocund independence

Warred against a god's restrictions; with our weapons of precision
We attacked the barren beauty of a beatific vision,
Aristotle-like we argued to applaud all human reasons
But He smote us - how He smote us - and condemned us to a
                                                                            season
Of interpreting the letters of His persecutor, Paul,
Whose love was pain, whose life was death, whose rising was his
                                                                            fall.

Lobotomised we shun the things our intellects thought good
And wait with geriatric teeth to nibble at the food
Of angels, that rejoice upon our reconciliation,
(Our tongues can all but tell the taste of transubstantiation);
Now Solomon concedes to us, philosophy's own schools
Are like an infant's play-books and we're happy to be fools
Who've parted with our learning for the honour of receiving
The stigmata of a lunatic, besotted and believing
That a mouthful of contrition can turn graveyards into glory,
We've traded Dostoyevsky for a simple little story

Of fisherman gone polymath, of murderer turned saint,
Of leopard lying down with lamb and none to think if quaint,
Or orchestrated angels paying tribute to a birth,
Of corpses drawing breath again and wandering the earth.
All this and more with bread we take, accepting it as meat,
Paul is the toast of idiots, and humbled at his feet
We've learned to say: 'adoro te,' with heart as well as tongue,
We've swallowed every paradox we scorned when we were young;
Since death is just a breath away, and Sartre makes us sick,
We shuffle through Corinthians and thank the Lord we're thick.

Frank Mc Donald

A Fool's Response

What God is this whose mind Paul knew?
That Paul who saw The Light so late
He grew, like sudden converts do,
Fanatic and could scarcely wait
To stop the world and set it back
On his new straight and narrow track.

I fear a missionary's zeal
May blind him to the obvious
For often, where his Faith would heal,
His dogma only brings distress,
And rules laid down with doctrine's rod
Exceed what men demand of god.

And what of men who see this earth
And each brief life through lovers' eyes?
Is it enough they treat with mirth
Creation's jests and churchy lies;
They need no gods nor yet a Paul
To prove the folly of It all.

Alex Smith

Cur Venisti, Proserpina?

So it is spring and you will bring
New flowers born of tears,
And you will court an old man's heart
And fashion hope from fears.
With soft deceit you will defeat
His sober protestations,
Setting him down, absurd old clown,
To sip your brief libations.

Why have you come to make him dream
Of lands beyond his knowing?
Why do you hurt his tired heart
With hope, when it is growing

Too late to love the things that move
Youth's hedonistic school?
Why should you want cruelly to taunt
An old, untutored fool?

Your pleasing blooms come from the tombs
Beyond the Stygian river;
Your green displays last only days,
Regret remains forever;
The whole world knows your floral shows,
The fragrance on your breath,
Merely conceal in vernal veil
The concubine of Death.

Tell artless boys of savage joys,
And fill their minds with madness;
Let ancients be who do not see
A world beyond their sadness.

Do not confuse with wondrous news
Old lips too cracked to sing.
Leave them alone to sigh and groan,
O heartless, heartless Spring!

Frank Mc Donald

Inner City Primavera

Groped by the caretaker down in the basement,
did as he told her because she was shy.
Flowers all faded, hair covered in coal dust,
too young to fight him, she only could cry.
Left by her mother who worked in the country.
Played in the park picking daisies alone.
Frantic, her mother searched for her daughter.
Panicked at last called the law on the phone.
No one could find the small girl in the cellar,
only one man had the key to that lock.
When he released her she went to the stairway
knowing the lift never worked in their block.
Took her two hours to climb eighteen storeys
up that dark shaft full of garbage and dirt.
Weak with not eating or drinking, she faltered,
crept like an insect, dishonoured and hurt.
Wished she had never accepted his present,
knew in her heart she must see him again.
Up in the tower her mother, despairing,
wreathed in dead poppies, was turned half insane.
Then the door opened and in came her daughter,
ran to her arms in the usual way.
Touched by the sun, withered plants in the window
blossomed at once celebrating the day.

Jenny Morris

Proserpina Discouraged

A bronchial croaking permeates the air
As Proserpina leaves her creaking bed.
The fever's gone, but energies are spare
And she is feeling less alive than dead.

The underworld is at its bleakest hour.
A plague pervades the atmosphere and she
Would like to leave, but seems to lack the power.
She needs to climb to earth and verdancy.

She searches in the corners of her room
For bright attire, but when she puts it on
It quenches any colour and the gloom
Assaults her sight and all she looks upon.

She turns to pots to animate her face,
But rouge enhances hollows round her eyes.
Where there were dimples lines have grown apace.
In place of laughter there are only sighs.

She grips the ladder, makes to reach a rung,
But as she mounts her weak resolve recedes.
The world is cold, her withers have been wrung,
Another week in bed is what she needs.

Patricia V Dawson

And Still Persephone Returns

Grey rimmed, I yawn, raise my bedraggled head
And peer out from my snowy eiderdown,
To mark where biting winter winds have shed
The icy jewels of fill-dyke's frosty crown.

The naked arms of trees thrash in the blast
And rake the steely vastness of the sky;
While Earth awaits the breaking of her fast
I must be deaf to sleep's sweet lullaby.

I hear the moans of numerous mortal men
Who pray for warmth and light to stir the land,
So that the fields may flourish once again;
And it shall come to pass at my command.

I shield my eyes against the dawning light,
Perhaps my sight is fading with the round
Of centuries of war and urban blight;
I feel much safer when I'm underground.

Enough complaining, there is work to do -
No time to sit around and feel depressed -
And I must make this old Earth look like new:
Great Zeus' daughter will not fail the test.

Maureen A Jeffs

Overdue

When the lift is out of order
(Pluto cannot get the spares),
And your horn of plenty seems to weigh a ton,
You must grit your teeth and bear it
As you climb those endless stairs,
For the Cycle of the Seasons has begun.

It's been hell down here this winter
With our heating on the blink,
Thirteen weeks is just as much as I can stand,
I'll be glad to reach the surface
Well away from sulphur stink,
And go back to helping mother on the land.

Temple priests no doubt will grumble
If I'm nowhere to be seen
And still missing an official opening date,
Then they'll offer blithe excuses
For the Earth not turning green
And resign themselves to Spring appearing late.

But rude plebs who execrate me
And refuse to sacrifice,
Change allegiance, having given me up for lost,
Will be taught a simple lesson -
That betrayal has its price -
When I dust their crops with sharp, untimely frost.

Brian Mitchell

Sloth: a Theory

Back in the days before the world grew cold,
When red was prefect on the schoolroom map,
It was a matter of some care to mould
The character of every little chap.
The goal, imparted at each mother's knee,
Was Effortless Superiority.

To get one's double first was quite okay,
But striving for it could be social death.
One might excel at games, but not betray
The slightest sign of being out of breath.
The gifted amateur, that's what was sought,
His brilliance more or less an afterthought.

Times change; and now the island race remains
Superior to no one very much.
Perhaps our pop groups have it on the Danes;
Perhaps our army might outrank the Dutch;
But on the whole we'd like to be allowed
To settle for survival with the crowd.

Yet ancient manners find it hard to die,
Although their owners may be down at the heel.
Despite our failure to be C B Fry,
We still aspire to half that beau ideal:
Superiority's beyond us far,
But effortless we can be; and we are.

Noel Petty

Darling

Unfold the deckchair, bring some lemonade.
Oh . . . don't forget my *Literary Review*.
Do move that awning . . . weeny bit more shade -
Isn't the sky a heavenly shade of blue?
The cricket dear? Oh, just let's skip the match.
It's quite a walk my dear . . . and that steep hill -
There is a programme on, that we could watch -
You know on damp grass, how I catch a chill.
It isn't that I'm idle. After all
We had the Smyths the other day for tea
And then that Mrs Simpson came to call.
she really *is* - a bit too much for me.

Be this not Sloth and this upon me proved,
I never writ and no man ever loafed.

Ralph Stephenson

The Sloth

Sluggishly suspended in the jungles of Brazil,
There is a shaggy monster who deserves a better press,
For he offers us a model we'd do nicely to fulfil
And he is the perfect answer for executives with stress.

But we've slandered him and numbered him in Seven Deadly Sins,
Full six of which need effort and are foreign to a sloth.
He's more at home with napping cats and basking terrapins
Than with avarice, pride, gluttony, lust, cov'tousness and wrath.

You needn't hit the bottle when your bright idea's vetoed,
Nor have a heart attack because the traffic's bad in Town.
Just contemplate a jungle full of creatures that are three-toed,
Smiling happily in hardwood trees they hang from upside-down.

Move more slowly in the morning when the rat-race is compelling.
Let that meeting start without you; why not stay in bed a while?
Ignore tomorrow: all the doom the papers are foretelling;
Become a sleepy creature with a beatific smile.

Victoria Thompson

Not Today

You could - but not today - do anything:
Begin a novel, start a restaurant,
Learn Arabic, restore a Gothic folly, sing
Tosca, or conquer Everest on a jaunt.
The world is all before you - but today,
Like yesterday, its options slither back.
Here in couch-comforts and thick dust you'll stay
While unconnected images amuse your slack
And flaccid dreams. Why shine in use
When doing nothing will suffice? Why strain?
Czech lager and perfunctory self-abuse
Trundles each day along its rutted lane.
No thoughts, beliefs: these absences are both
Beginning and destructive end of Sloth.

D A Prince

England

I travel through a strange and alien land,
Unwilling to converse or understand,
The people that I meet and things I see
Are blissfully inscrutable to me;
I seek no explanation as I go,
Luxuriously unconcerned to know.

Along each highway never-ending pass
Those motivations of the doing class:
Ambition vengeance vanity and gain,
With scruple trailing in the outer lane.
I skulk among the roadside undergrowth
In company with apathy and sloth.

Then in a crumbling palace, once alight,
I see the future of our nation's might,
With soldiers lawyers politicians all,
Gavotting at the abdication ball;
While poets, idly dreaming in the dark,
Illuminate our world and tenure mark.

Robert Marks

Ode to Idleness

Sweet slothfulness, that deadly bliss
Which makes the angels weep,
Seeps softly - Oh to hell with this,
I'm going back to sleep.

Richard Charles

The Poetry, Not the Poet

He felt a burning need to write,
so left his job. He borrowed ink
and pen and paper. He composed
in poverty, with not a bite
to eat, and only air to drink:
What Poetry from his pen flowed!

He found an Editor, who smiled
on him, and gave him column space.
His reputation slowly grew.
In time, a slim book was compiled,
but didn't suit the critics taste
when, in its turn, it was reviewed:

'This man has never known pain
of pregnancy or parturition,
being masculine by birth.
Nor has he endured the reign
of dictatorial oppression
over his small patch of earth.

He has not suffered torture, nor
the secret loss of those he loves,
taken silently by night,
nor lived the hall of civil war,
where sister hawks fight brother doves
with cries of 'Freedom!' for the right

to rule the land as they see fit.
He is not Jewish, Black or Gay,
He fits no clear minority;
He is not mad, he is not sick,
or handicapped in any way;
He has no right to poetry.'

He read this verdict, which discerned
no good in what he had to say.
He read the spite between the lines
but carried on, quite unconcerned,
to answer in the simplest way,
still being read in latter times.

Robert Hart

Spite and Envy

I am an ornamental fish
inside a garden pond,
and genuinely do not wish
to see the world beyond.

I'm told that, in the silver sea,
a great white shark may bask;
but why should greatness bother me?
Indeed, why do I ask?

My cronies underneath the pads
are similarly bright:
these claims to fame are foolish fads,
like us, mere sparks of light.

The adulation of a whale,
coelacanth or eel,
forgets our tiny, perfect scale:
we're just as fine, we feel.

These monsters of the ocean move
through time like king or queen:
what have they got, what do they prove
about the current scene?

I'm like a poet, underpaid,
expected to feel faint
when Tennyson is on parade.
You'd think he was a saint.

The same with Shakespeare: I prefer
to hear my fishy sound,
to be a tiny, brilliant blur,
swim round and round and round.

Bill Greenwell

The Great McGonagall

In highland garb he led the cavalcade,
To wild acclaim bestrode the circus ring,
As brave men fled his flashing blade, portrayed
The battle triumph of a Scottish king.

For thus the famous poet entertainer,
Heroic music hall and tavern turn,
Enthusiastic alcohol abstainer,
Performed his epic Bruce at Bannockburn.

Though ever mocked by educated fools
And plagued by hooligans and hangers-on,
He stood aloof from petty ridicules
And thought himself as good as Tennyson.

With precious little honour and less pay,
Oppressed by magistrates and poverty,
He made immortal railway bridge of Tay
And brought its only fame to mean Dundee.

Now all around the world his works are seen,
His lines are quoted still, his rhymes enthral:
As played by Peter Sellers on the screen,
The Great Sir William Topaz McGonagall.

Robert Marks

John Keats

Of course it was consumption: this is fact.
Blood, flecking sputum, bubbling in the chest,
The spectre-haunted pallor, ravaged rest,
All Severn's evidence - he never lacked

A friend, even at the end. A textbook case -
His brother had it too: hereditary.
Nothing to do with rhyme or poetry.
His classic symptoms stare you in the face.

And yet below Rome's Spanish Steps there cling
Shadows of stains, faint sourness in the breath,
A feverish chorus whispering early death
Was ushered forward by the critics string

Of bludgeoning attacks. Their words, their pen,
Wielding for writers mortal poisoning power,
Whipped on the greedy virus to devour
His shivering life, and gnaw his lungs again.

Gouging, their mean nibs steeled with bitter spite,
Scoring with ignorance, flailing for greed
The poet's heart, his mirror, secret need
To justify his deepest wish - to write

And write as no man wrote before, to claim
A sheaf of words, new patternings, a quarter -
And not just one so faintly writ in water -
But staked out as his own, a lasting name.

D A Prince

The Price of Envy

Cursed be the bard whose verses have been read.
The mob ignores his books upon the shelf
and not content to leave him safely dead,
it turns its ire upon the man himself.

His fellow scribblers find it worth their while
to denigrate his all too easy fame,
investigate his loves, his lack of style
and call his life parochial and tame.

Biographies invade the Sunday press,
where, serialised, his vices are laid bare
for all to pry, particularly less
accomplished poets, struggling to be there

when handouts, honours, praise and grand esteem
are meted out, but when is this to be?
Where lurks the jury? Only in a dream
could such a band of arbiters agree.

No, fame goes hand in hand with hate and spite.
This triple marriage will not break or bend.
It hovers, overshadowing delight.
The till proclaims the poet in the end.

Patricia V Dawson

A Qualified Toast

The Ladies, God bless them. I think you will find
that under the frills there's more matter than mind.

They say they're the salt of the earth, but we know
they're the sugar and spice of our fabulous show.

Keep them out of the smoke room, we like them instead
in the kitchen, the larder, the nursery and bed.

They may have ambitions, but bless their sweet hearts,
we prefer to regard them as mothers or tarts.

They are not so creative as talented men
with an opera score or a brush or a pen.

They are there to give birth and to answer our needs,
so that we can reward them with axes and beads.

They must strive to be pretty, insouciant and slim
and anything else that appeals to a him.

We can grow a pot belly, decide when we'll shave
and drink ourselves happily into the grave.

But they must be sober in order to drive
and be healthy and wealthy so we can survive.

We are watching the darlings. If they're out of step,
it's our place to correct them with vigour and pep.

They have entered the club and the boardroom and bar.
Now they're into the Church, which is going too far.

So here's to the ladies, provided they stay
in the background, the wings, or the family way.

Patricia V Dawson

The Wife

My heart is like a chocolate cake
Whose rich aroma fills the air,
My heart is like a casserole
I dream of as I mount the stair.
My heart is like banana split
With reddest strawberries and cream,
And when in conjoined love we fit
My kitchen mingles with your dream.

Bring me a bowl in which the gold
Of grapes and apricots is seen
While in my kitchen I unfold
The mysteries of haute cuisine,
And you, my love, shall be the first
To taste my dedicated art
And in my tender meats discern
The flavour of a loving heart.

Richard Blomfield

Footnotes

I love uniquely you; I do not love,
as some austere philosophers have claimed,
in you rare essence at a high remove,
the classic virtues by your beauty framed.
Wild worship's what your sensual self suggests,
not reverence of a cold Platonic Form:
I hunger only for your proud, round breasts;
I know your eyes, incomparably warm.

But if I seem obtuse or simply blind,
failing to see pure womanhood shine through
your fleshly filter, yet I sometimes find
in other women elements of you:
and so each face on which may fall my gaze
becomes a footnote on your scroll of praise.

David Shields

Index of Poets

Balch, Barbara	102
Blake, Alanna	15, 34, 52, 55, 71, 94
Blomfield, Richard	54, 138
Browning, Stella	82
Butler, Joan	27
Caldwell, Roger	99, 114
Charles, Richard	115, 130
Chown, Helen	87
Cramp, H St G	116
Dawson, Patricia	85, 122, 136, 137
Fitzpatrick, Eva	46
Forbes-Handley, A	51
Forsyth, Helen	56
Graves, Richard	96
Greenwell, Bill	57, 62, 133
Griffin, Paul	3, 7, 29, 45, 60, 86, 91, 93
Hart, Robert	131
Harvey, G R	106
Hopkins, Tim	70, 98
Imlay, Elizabeth	76
Jeffs, Maureen	58, 81, 123
Johnson, Austin	65
Jones, Anne	25
Knapp, S	20
Lloyd, Myfanwy	89
Lyons, Kate	17
Mallet, Katie	63, 67
Maranka, M	42
Marfell-Harris, C F	75
Marks, Robert	32, 129, 134
Marr, Herbert	4, 11
Mc Donald, Frank	19, 38, 50, 53, 61, 79, 111, 117, 119
McGregor, Sheila	21
Melvin, Maureen	14
Miller, Christian	1

Mitchell, Brian	26, 124
Morris, Jenny	69, 121
Neville, Jill	88
Nicholson, Philip A	13, 28, 30, 35, 48, 73, 83, 108, 113
Norman, P	41
Pearson, C	49
Perry, Robert	64
Petty, Noel	77, 109, 125
Porter, Charles	92
Prince, Alison	107
Prince, D A	31, 40, 72, 95, 97, 128, 135
Rodgers, Don	74
Sadik, Elizabeth	101
Shields, David	139
Sinclair, Angus	112
Skelton, Robin	5, 9
Smit, Adelgonda	23
Smith, Alex	118
Spalding, Sarah	16
Spreader, Mortimer	103
Staniforth, Lindsay	59
Stephenson, Ralph	126
Thompson, Victoria	127
Turner, Katherine	78
Walton, Ian	37
Warbis, Allan	84, 110
Ward, Gay	39
Waters, Charles	33
Welby, Edward	47, 105
Williams, Mr and Mrs J	18
Wilson, Frances	2